Spirit To Heal

A Journey to Spiritual Healing with Cancer

With very best wishes

[signature]

[signature] Michael Torosian

Michael H. Torosian, M.D.

Veruschka R. Biddle, Ph.D.

Spirit Press International

Published by Spirit Press International

Grateful acknowledgement is made for permission to reprint material
from the following texts:

Reprinted by permission of Baker Book House Co., Grand Rapids:
quotations from *12,000 Inspirational Quotations; A Treasury of
Spiritual Insights and Practical Wisdom* edited by Frank S. Mead,
Copyright © 1965.

Reprinted by permission of The Continuum International Publishing
Group, New York: excerpt from *Invitation to Love* by Thomas Keating,
Copyright © 1996.

Reprinted by permission of Random House, Inc., New York: excerpt
from *The Doctor and the Soul* by Viktor E. Frankl, Copyright © 1980.

Reprinted by permission of Victory House Publishers, Tulsa: excerpt
adapted from *Healing of the Wounded Spirit* by J Sandford and P
Sandford, Copyright © 1985.

The content of this book is intended for informational purposes only
and is not to be used as a basis for medical advice, including but not
limited to diagnosis or treatment, of any condition. The names,
circumstances and case histories used in this book have been altered to
preserve the confidentiality of individuals.

Cover Photo by Steven Begleiter
Cover Design by AXIS Visual
ISBN 0-9729419-0-8   Printed and bound in the U.S.A

We dedicate this book to our parents
Harry and *Dorothy Torosian*
and *Heinz* and *Erna Dettmar,*
Michael's sister *Alice McCollam*
and to *Captain Edward* and *Janet Biddle*
may they always be with us.
And to our children *Justin, Davina, Juliana* and *Marcus*
may they always be blessed.

Contents

Preface

We have had the opportunity through years of clinical practice to understand the impact that the diagnosis of cancer can have on one's life. Our hope is that this book will help our readers discover the incredible resources, strength, beauty and depth of the human spirit. We believe that God has created our body, mind and spirit to function in unity and that the human spirit can sustain us even when our physical or mental health fails. Our spirit is unique and delicately created and needs to be nurtured with love, compassion and kindness. The human spirit has an innate wisdom to guide and strengthen us and can never be destroyed, not even by death. Our spirit is immortal and will return to God, our Creator.

The purpose of this book is to deepen our spiritual relationship with God and others and to realize the power of our spiritual strength during times of illness, such as cancer. We have written this book from our Judeo-Christian perspective and do not intend to exclude anyone from a different faith or religion – our hope is that everyone can reference this text to the God of their own belief and understanding. We speak in this book mainly about spirituality and are not advocating any particular church, religion, or teaching. When I started to integrate spirituality into the fields of medicine and psychotherapy in 1989, questions abounded at that time. Today the integration of spirituality and medicine is gaining acceptance and recognition in many academic and clinical institutions. Although modern psychology and psychiatry focus primarily on the healing forces within their patients, the Spiritual Integrated Approach combines the healing forces of the human body, mind and spirit with the power and love of God. We believe that all healing ultimately comes from God and that healing prayer can release these forces to achieve spiritual growth and support the healing process.

This book introduces a new way of understanding the human spirit and its incredible capacity to strengthen the body and mind during times of illness and struggle. The purpose and essence of this therapy is to open one to the unlimited love, power and grace of God and to affirm that we are not alone in times of illness. This therapy recognizes the importance of the physical, spiritual, emotional and intellectual dimensions of human life.

The Spiritual Integrated Approach brings a unique perspective that science alone cannot provide. By uniting the laws of science and the mysteries of faith, a new and powerful force emerges from deep within our spirit that reaches beyond human understanding. Our spirituality creates hope and faith which are divinely inspired and have tremendous healing potential. Along our spiritual journey, we are confronted with many difficult life challenges and we never face these challenges alone – God is always with us. Our struggles and burdens can be surrendered to God and He will sustain us through even the most difficult times of our life. We have the great opportunity to grow and to transcend these worldly problems with the strength of our spirit. The human spirit is eternal and our ultimate purpose is to return to the One who created us.

Our aim is that this book will be a source of hope and inspiration to cancer patients around the world. Everyone possesses the **spirit to heal** that creates a peace and serenity that surpasses all human understanding. We believe that it is God's will to have love and peace among His people of all religions.

This book does not present theological principles or religious doctrine but demonstrates the love of God that has sustained humanity since creation. We believe that the use of prayer, faith and forgiveness integrated with traditional medicine is a powerful combination. Our purpose is to help people who are suffering from this illness to find hope and strength within their spirit. There is something in all of us that requires healing, our whole world is in desperate need for healing and returning to the love of God so that we can live in peace.

A number of wonderful people have encouraged and inspired us during our training. We would especially like to acknowledge our mentors Dr. Jonathan Rhoads (MHT) and Dr. Eugene D'Aquili (VRB) who have taught us the importance and art of compassion in medicine and who have guided and prepared us for integrating the fields of spirituality and medicine. Our friend and colleague Dr. Michelle Battistini has motivated us to write this book. We value our friendship with Dr. Andrew Newberg whose groundbreaking research in neurophysiology supports our work on the impact of prayer and spirituality on the human mind and body. We extend our gratitude for the support, love and prayers of our friends and family.

I would like to express my gratitude to my friend and co-author Michael Torosian for his brilliance, encouragement, and outstanding ability to see this project through from start to finish. His hard work was responsible for the development not only of this book, but also of our seminars, courses and retreats which have already helped hundreds of people. Without him this work would not have been completed. I thank Michael especially for his continuous support, loyalty, and most of all for believing in the importance of integrating spirituality and medicine in the treatment of patients with cancer – VRB.

My sincerest appreciation is gratefully extended to Veruschka Biddle whose steadfast commitment, diligence and great proficiency was essential to the successful completion of this work. Her lifelong devotion and belief in the power of prayer and spirituality is inspiring to all around her. Her pioneering work in this field has helped and will continue to help many patients overcome some of the most difficult times of their lives. Veruschka is a true friend, devoted teacher, and superb clinician who will undoubtedly continue to make great contributions in this field for many years to come – MHT.

Finally we would like to express our gratitude to our patients, who have taught and given us so much and who have trusted us in the most difficult times of their lives. We would especially like to express our deep appreciation to Sister Rose who has opened her heart and life to us. She exemplifies the love of God, the power of prayer and the strength of the human spirit and shows us how one can make the impossible possible. There will always be more to discover about the beauty and mystery of the human spirit – this work is an ongoing and exciting quest. We are devoted to this work, and our hope is that no one should suffer the despair and hopelessness of cancer ever again.

Above all we thank God for His guidance and inspiration and for allowing us to bring peace, love and hope to His People – and we pray and hope that this book brings healing, blessings, hope and strength to all who suffer from cancer and their loved ones. May God's blessing and guidance be with them and may they always feel His presence.

CHAPTER 1

A TIME OF CRISIS

"Faith is the force of life."

Leo Tolstoy (1828 – 1910)

Conventional medicine has limitations – spirituality does not! By reading this book, you are about to embark on a journey that could change your life forever. Spiritual Integrated Treatment is a technique powerful enough to heal the human spirit and soul. It is now evident that the mind, body and spirit do not work in isolation but are connected at every level. Prehistoric man knew this thousands of years ago and used spirituality, faith, and religion to achieve healing. Recent pioneering research into the realm of prayer and the biologic function of the human brain has confirmed these ancient beliefs. We can now re-unite the powerful forces of science and spirituality to achieve spiritual healing of patients with the most feared disease worldwide – cancer.

Patients with cancer often experience intense psychological and spiritual reactions to the diagnosis and ongoing fear of progression of this disease. Millions of cancer patients suffer from symptoms ranging from nightmares to headaches to anxiety to depression. Profound consequences can include withdrawal from family and friends, extreme sadness, anxiety, anger, guilt, pessimism, sexual problems and emotional numbness.   Patients can experience anger toward God and feelings of guilt, punishment, and abandonment. Questions arise such as "Why does God allow me to suffer?" Often one reaches a crisis of faith and can experience a complete loss of trust in God. The fear of death and dying, wondering what happens after death, concern about their loved ones left behind – these are difficult challenges facing the cancer patient. Life does not prepare us for that sudden traumatic event that begins when one first hears the diagnosis of "cancer."

You will see how cancer can be the story of courage, determination, resilience, and the ultimate triumph of the human spirit. Today there is much cause for hope. People with cancer can be greatly helped and many, many cancer patients can be cured.   Yet, cancer has the potential to cause great emotional chaos and to shatter the soul – but, there is no reason for anyone to suffer this devastating effect of cancer ever again. We have developed the Spiritually Integrated Treatment approach, an innovative therapy that can relieve the great emotional and spiritual turmoil caused by cancer. This approach can help people overcome the fear, anxiety and despair of cancer and achieve profound healing toward a new journey of joyful and peaceful living.

The power of love and the human spirit are the prime sources of everything good in life. Love and spirituality can empower us to live a life full of peace and serenity, meaning and purpose.   True healing of the human spirit and soul can be attained by drawing on these enormous resources of power. These magnificent forces can overcome illness and heal the scars of emotional pain and hopelessness so many cancer patients experience. We have chosen the remarkable journey of Sister Rose to demonstrate the strong message of survival, crisis of faith, power of hope and ultimate triumph over cancer. Sister Rose, a Franciscan nun, is among the most radiant human beings one could ever find in life. She radiates happiness and love and embodies hope and faith – but, Sister Rose also suffered greatly at the hands of the disease known as "cancer." Her story shines like a ray of sunshine for all to follow in their journey to achieve complete spiritual healing.

Sister Rose is now 81 years old and as vibrant, creative and inspirational as ever. She was diagnosed with breast cancer 4 ½ years ago and her initial reaction was one of total shock. How could she have developed breast cancer? She had no symptoms and had no family history of breast cancer. She lived a life of devotion and commitment to God. How could this have happened to her? But, the story only begins here as, during her preoperative evaluation, a second tumor was found growing inside her heart! The heart tumor was a rare growth called a myxoma and was not related to her newly discovered breast cancer in any way. Now she was really devastated – not one, but two tumors which required serious treatment. Although the heart tumor was benign, it could cause serious complications, including stroke and even sudden death. How was she to cope with this shocking turn of events? Her doctors recommended open heart surgery to remove the heart tumor as soon as possible. Then, she still needed to face surgery for her breast cancer. How was Sister Rose to react? Would her physical strength and spiritual power enable her to endure these treatments? Would her emotional or spiritual state be traumatized forever? Would her life-long beliefs or her faith in God be weakened? Or, perhaps, would she be strengthened by these challenging life crises?

This dramatic story embodies the devastating impact that cancer can have on an individual – and, as you will learn, the power of spirituality in overcoming cancer. Sister Rose's journey became the most significant time in her life. A time of intense anguish that opened the door to a new inner freedom, a new hope and even more creativity. As you will see, she gained much by living through the challenges of the most difficult time of her life. A story of courage that will empower others, her journey shows that light and darkness, hope and despair, love and fear are never far apart – and that true spiritual freedom often requires a sudden transformation of one's thoughts, reactions, motives, and actions. You will see how Sister Rose and other cancer patients are empowered to survive cancer with the support of faith, hope, love and spirituality.

Finding hope and meaning in difficult times is a miracle in itself and a sign of God's love and presence. At times when our pain is the greatest, we have a wonderful opportunity to lift our eyes to heaven and invite God to help us through the storm. Cancer instills so much fear, anxiety and uncertainty in the spirit of its victims that it challenges the will of our soul, our very essence. We now have the power, strength and conviction to overcome these formidable challenges and to free ourselves from this troublesome burden.

It is not just the physical aspects of this disease, but these fears and uncertainties of cancer that can destroy one's life. These intense emotional responses affect the body's ability to heal. Healing requires transformation and spirituality is the way we connect and communicate with God to overcome these fears and to combat the despair and hopelessness of cancer. Suppressed grief, guilt, unforgiveness, bitterness, resentment and self hate take a tremendous toll on our emotional equilibrium and on our spirit. Releasing these destructive feelings is an important part of healing. We cannot heal without the power of love – love for

God, love for others and love for ourselves. Forgiveness releases a healing energy and empowers the human spirit. A life shattered by suffering such as cancer can easily destroy one's spirit – we must rise above that emotional pain to transform weakness into strength, fear into hope, and passivity into action to heal from the depths of suffering.

Personal histories are used throughout this book to demonstrate the impact and success of the Spiritual Integrated Treatment in helping patients survive cancer. Scientific research has shown clear evidence of interaction between our physical bodies and our spiritual existence. In fact, receptors have been identified on cells within our immune system and within the brain itself that enable these two powerful systems to freely interact. Every thought, feeling and impulse that we experience can alter our immune system which in turn can affect the way we think, feel, and heal from illness. Prayer, meditation and spirituality have dramatic and profound changes on the function of our brains – pioneering research into the workings of the human mind during spiritual experiences are fascinating and will be shown to you. We have combined the elements of science, the compassionate care of patients, and the healing forces of the human mind and spirit to achieve healing with our spiritual treatment approach.

Ancient medicine was practiced by religious and spiritual leaders throughout the history of mankind and shows a historical connection between mind and body (Carmichael AG, Ratzan RM, 1991). The Sumerian-Babylonian-Assyrian civilization (2500 BC) searched for internal causes of disease – i.e., within one's body. The early Hebrew culture focused on disease as punishment for disobeying or contradicting God's laws. In India, Ayurveda, one of the oldest of all the health sciences, proposed that health and well-being required a balance between mind, body and spirit, and disease represented a disruption of this balance. Philosophy, spirituality and religion were known to be important forces of healing in this ancient medical practice as early as 4000 – 3000 BC. Essentially every human culture has used a form of prayer during stress, disease or death. In fact, rituals were used when burying the dead as long as 100,000 years ago.

As science progressed through many centuries, however, a great separation occurred between scientific culture and spirituality. Great progress was made in science – but science lost its ancient connection to spirituality and religion. We have carefully integrated the fields of psychotherapy, surgical oncology, and the latest scientific research in the field of spirituality and brain function to develop the Spiritual Integrated Treatment. This technique starts from the diagnosis of cancer and treats all aspects of cancer – physical, emotional, psychologic and spiritual. This treatment is unique and has shown great success in treating patients with many types of cancer. The Spiritual Integrated Treatment approach reunites the two great fields of science and spirituality to eliminate the devastating emotional and spiritual suffering so many cancer patients experience. Health care professionals need to learn how to integrate the fields of medicine, psychiatry and spirituality to truly heal the human body, mind and spirit. Our goal is to practice and teach one how to integrate the fields of science and spirituality to achieve the greatest possible success in treating each and every cancer patient.

Cancer strikes fear into the hearts and minds of its victims. This disease is the second leading killer of people in the United States and one of the leading causes of death worldwide. Almost immediately the cancer patient is faced with a complexity of overwhelming emotions and thoughts. Traumatized and in a state of uncertainty, the newly diagnosed cancer patient must try to cope with this life-changing event. Medical procedures and interventions can trigger even more fear and deep suffering. Most physicians today don't fully acknowledge the despair and suffering that patients feel at the level of the soul – in fact, the emotional and psychologic aspects of cancer are often neglected. Medical science can successfully eliminate the physical pain but commonly ignores the pain deep within one's soul – a pain that can be much more destructive and debilitating than physical suffering. One in the midst of a crisis such as cancer, however, has a unique opportunity – that is, to transform the suffering and pain into a deeper dimension of spiritual awareness, purpose and insight that leads to peacefulness and healing. The Spiritual Integrative Approach teaches one to shift one's fear and anxiety to courage, hope and peacefulness. Suffering, whether physical or emotional, teaches us to reach deep within ourselves to strive for a higher purpose in life.

Cancer can strike anyone at any time at any age – it knows no limits or boundaries. Cancer can develop in any organ or tissue in the body and has the unique ability to recur locally and to spread, or metastasize, to distant parts of the body. It is this characteristic of distant spread or metastasis that distinguishes cancer from all other diseases – this important feature of cancer is also responsible, in large part, for the fear, anxiety, despair, uncertainty, unpredictability and hopelessness of its victims. The mere threat of metastasis in the cancer patient can cause severe anxiety, gloom and significant depression.

Questions of guilt often arise in cancer patients trying to explain why they developed cancer. Patients who eat a healthy diet, exercise regularly, and abstain from smoking and excessive alcohol intake often cannot understand how or why they developed cancer. However, anyone can develop cancer. Cancer growth and progression is a complex process but is ultimately caused by changes, or mutations, in the genes within a cell, the basic unit of our bodies. These genetic mutations can be caused by many different biologic mechanisms and pathways; some are inherited but most are chance, or sporadic, events. Once a cell has become cancerous in this way, it develops into a tumor by unregulated growth and can spread to other parts of the body. Why one individual develops cancer and another with similar genetic and environmental risk factors does not, is unknown and poses a critical question for today's cancer researchers.

Regardless of the biologic cause of cancer, quality of life is greatly influenced by the strength and determination of one's faith and conviction. Spirituality has an important role to play in the healing process of cancer and can dramatically improve quality of life. Uncertainty, fear, and unpredictability of cancer are major causes of emotional and psychosocial trauma caused by this disease state. Once cancer has been diagnosed, many questions about this disease and its treatments suddenly arise. Can the cancer be cured? Has the cancer spread? What treatments are needed to fight the cancer? Will I need surgery? Will I need radiation therapy? Will I need chemotherapy? Will I be sick from the treatments, especially radiation therapy and chemotherapy? Is my cancer contained? Did I do something to cause my cancer? Are my family members at risk to develop cancer?

The initial response to the diagnosis of cancer is often one of disbelief. The diagnosis hits one abruptly and traumatically – being diagnosed with cancer is like walking across the street and being hit by an oncoming car. Cancer, like an unexpected traumatic accident, changes one's life forever. The cancer diagnosis instantly becomes the focal point of one's medical history for all future examinations, x-ray tests and medical interventions. The fear of discovering recurrent cancer or metastatic disease may fade with time but is always present to some extent in the mind of the cancer patient at subsequent examinations.

Conventional medical therapy is the mainstay of cancer treatment and consists of surgery, radiation therapy, and chemotherapy in various combinations. Conventional medicine, however, typically treats the physical aspects of cancer and ignores its psychologic and spiritual components. Beyond the traditional cancer therapies, supportive measures can be used effectively to improve the quality of life and, perhaps, length of survival of the cancer patient. Nutrition support, pain relief, physical therapy, occupational therapy, speech therapy, and various complimentary medical therapies can contribute to the well being of the cancer patient. Spirituality is one of the most powerful, but underutilized, means to improve one's strength, energy level, social interactions, family participation, and joy of living. Spirituality is an adjunct, not a competitor, to conventional medical therapy and has tremendous potential to improve the life of the cancer patient.

By combining science, oncology and Spiritual Integrated Psychotherapy, we have the greatest potential to achieve healing, hope, love and peace. The integration of spirituality into the art of medicine is extremely powerful for improving health outcome. Our goal is to treat the physical, emotional, and spiritual effects of cancer in the body, mind and spirit. Healing is a spiritual journey. There are lessons to be learned as we go through the stages of healing. Curing the physical aspect of disease is only one component of medical care; relieving the emotional and spiritual effects of cancer is just as essential to achieve complete healing of the cancer patient.

The devastating effects on one's physical, emotional, psychological and spiritual well being start immediately with the diagnosis of cancer – that single word "cancer" has tremendous impact on us. But these effects are felt not only by the patient, but also by his loved ones. We believe that all of these aspects of cancer must be confronted and defeated if one is truly going to survive this debilitating disease. Spiritual Integrated Treatment helps cancer patients live well and grow spiritually, finding comfort and strength in their conviction and faith in God. To promote healing in the cancer patient, we must acknowledge and release emotional and psychological stresses – our spiritual strength can create a world of peacefulness and serenity in the midst of potential chaos.

What are the physical effects of cancer and its associated treatments? The physical or somatic effects of cancer are widespread and can include weight loss, anorexia (decreased appetite), fatigue, fever, easy bruisability, bleeding, nausea, pain, shortness of breath, and many other symptoms. Conventional medical treatments, such as surgery, radiation therapy, and chemotherapy, play an important role in physically combating cancer. However, there are acute and often dramatic side effects from these cancer therapies. Surgical treatment of cancers can include removal of the breast, lung, prostate gland, female gynecologic organs, intestine, kidney, bladder, and portions of the head and neck to name a few. Such surgical procedures are associated with significant emotional overlay and leave not only physical but emotional and psychological scars.

Radiation therapy causes functional changes in internal organs, such as the bowel and bladder, and can cause skin discoloration, thickening and visible scarring. Some radiation effects are acute (i.e., time-limited) and others are chronic or long-lasting. Chemotherapy is typically the most dreaded treatment because of its whole body effects. Side effects can include hair loss, nausea, diarrhea, and symptoms of bone marrow suppression, such as fatigue, easy bruisability, and recurrent infection. Despite the common occurrence of adverse effects, cancer therapy is often pushed to the limits of human toxicity in an attempt to cure or control this devastating disease.

The power of spirituality is now being recognized as a potent adjunct to traditional medical therapies and must be unleashed to truly conquer cancer. Medical treatments alone are not sufficient to relieve the emotional devastation, fear and resentment that can affect the patient in many ways, especially spiritually. Fear, guilt, anger and disappointment are deeply rooted in the mind and spirit. The greatest repression of our human condition is not hostility or sexuality, as was thought a few years ago, but spirituality. When we are repressed spiritually, our lives are lacking love, hope, faith and peace. We feel fragile, vulnerable and deprived. We stay emotionally fixed or trapped in a state of emotional pain. Many of us repress, avoid or deny deep or complex feelings and, in this way, block spiritual awareness. The stress that is created by avoiding our deepest feelings places a tremendous toll on the human mind, body and spirit. Our quality of life, personal growth, and social relationships can be greatly enhanced by the positive power of spirituality.

The emotional toll of cancer and the harsh consequences of its medical treatments are great. Simply knowing that one has cancer and requires such treatments can cause feelings of grief, depression, loneliness, and despair. But it is in this time of deep suffering that we must focus on our innermost core to find strength to overcome these intense, debilitating emotions. We do not have absolute power over our cancer – but, we do have power over our mind and we have access to the unlimited power of our spirit at all times. As research has clearly shown, we only use a small portion of the mental potential of our brain in our daily thoughts – likewise, we use only a fraction of the spiritual power available to us at any time. Our spiritual resources are incredibly valuable and must not be forgotten, especially in times when they are needed the most.

Amazing things start to happen when we tune into our spiritual resources and strength. The power of love, hope, faith, and spirituality is intense and enduring. To love and to be loved is perhaps the single most important feature of being healthy – and being human. The clinical impact of spirituality on healing, coping, recovering and, at times, dealing with recurrence and death from cancer is a remarkable journey which you can take with us through the pages of this book – we will explore this incredible phenomenon together, and you can experience the tremendous power of spirituality. It can be a life-changing voyage for you.

The vast majority of studies and published clinical reports indicate that spirituality and religion have a clear and positive effect on one's recovery from illness. The biologic mechanisms linking spirituality to one's health have been programmed into the human brain over millions of years of evolution. The scientific evidence for this phenomenon is fascinating and was convincingly shown by recent, pioneering studies in the field of neurophysiology. During prayer and meditation, specific changes in brain activity have been documented by functional imaging studies (Newberg A, D'aquili E, Rause V, 2001). However, not every religious or deeply spiritual experience can be reduced to a chemical reaction or a precise biologic process within the brain. Spirituality remains somewhat ethereal, mysterious, and mystical – in fact, there are aspects of spirituality and religion that may never be fully understood.

We have the option of feeling lost and destroyed by cancer or in living in the power of God's love – it is our choice. Certain cancers, however, are particularly devastating to one's emotional and spiritual state of mind. For example, breast cancer and gynecologic cancers are especially harmful to women because of their significant connection to the state of femininity. Breast removal or loss of childbearing ability by removal of gynecologic organs carries obvious emotional trauma beyond the typical fears and concerns of the cancer itself. For men, prostate removal and its potential to cause impotence challenges their concept of manhood. Extensive surgery or radiation therapy of head and neck cancer can significantly alter appearance and body image of both men and women with adverse consequences on their personal, social and professional lives. In this way, significant psychologic, social and spiritual harm can result from cancer and its harsh therapy.

Confronting the physical, emotional and psychologic trauma of cancer can be disruptive to one's interpersonal relationships. Learning to love deeply and unconditionally is part of the spiritual journey to healing that will strengthen oneself and one's relationships. Personal relationships that were previously solid and strong can be severely tested -- and even broken if not properly nurtured. Struggles and challenges in such relationships can abruptly surface under the ominous burdens of cancer. Of course, some patients are able to meet these challenges with optimism and determination and can function in the face of adversity – others adapt in diverse and destructive ways when faced with the social stresses of cancer. In extreme cases, dysfunctional behavior can result, with the unfortunate person being incapacitated by the trauma of cancer. For example, Barbara is a 43-year-old woman who was devastated by depression and paralyzed with fear after being diagnosed with terminal cancer. Six weeks after starting to embrace her spiritual strength, her outlook on life dramatically changed, and her fear and depression remarkably diminished. She changed her life course forever and has achieved inner peace and renewed hope for the future. She has become an inspiration to her friends, family and other patients in her support group. Relying on her inner source of strength, she and many others like her can overcome the difficult challenges of cancer.

Spirituality is broadly defined and is clearly distinct from religion. Of course, religion and attendance at religious services can constitute spirituality – other definitions include faith in a Greater Power, renewed purpose in life, faith, trust, prayer, meditation and hope. Spirituality and faith can be severely questioned in the cancer patient – even those with the strongest beliefs in religion and spirituality, such as Sister Rose. The physical, emotional, and psychosocial trauma of cancer are constant challenges to one's basic spiritual beliefs – these challenges must be overcome to strengthen one's spirituality and to fully survive cancer. Our goal is to prevent the harmful and destructive consequences of cancer from affecting any cancer patient ever again.

Spiritual healing is an active, internal process that requires the careful analysis of one's attitudes, motives, memories, beliefs and desires – and a willingness to change any negative process that prevents our emotional, physical and spiritual recovery. Each one of us has a unique spirit – just like we each have a unique personality or genetic makeup. Being around someone who is spiritually awake and sensitive creates a healing environment and a reviving, therapeutic connection. Creativity, love, and the will to live have tremendous biologic impact on our health and well being.

Healing is a return to God's love – but, that may not mean a cure or a remission from cancer. The greatest gift is healing of the human spirit. A wonderful and successful life is not determined by one's physical health – moreover, physical death does not represent the end of our existence. We are enlightened to know that there is a greater life beyond the physical one we are living at this moment. God's love for us is greater than that and reaches beyond death. His Love is the greatest of all unions and one should not be fearful or afraid of suffering at death. All of our hardships, trials, illnesses and even our losses have the potential to help our spirit grow, deepen and strengthen – this may be the primary purpose for our physical existence on earth. We can and must use these opportunities, even the unwelcome ones like cancer, to nurture our spirit and soul. We will take you on an extraordinary journey – to understand this devastating illness known as "cancer", to focus your thoughts and emotions, and to discover the mystery of the mind-body-spirit connection. You can awaken your soul and experience a healing transformation of your spirit on this incredible journey!

CHAPTER 2

A TIME FOR COMPASSION

**"The best portion of a good man's life,
His little, nameless, unremembered acts
Of kindness and of love."**

William Wordsworth (1770 -1850)

Cancer is a devastating disease that touches everyone. We all know someone close to us who has cancer – a family member, a friend, a co-worker, or perhaps you. Despite all the great advances in cancer treatment, this disease remains a leading cause of death worldwide. Before the development of antibiotics in the mid-20th century, infectious diseases were the leading cause of mortality. The current epidemic is cancer.

The importance of spirituality in the healing process and for the doctor/patient relationship has been known for thousands of years. Aristotle believed and wrote in his teaching about the importance of the soul to maintain one's physical health (Ellis H, 2001). This ancient Greek scholar and philosopher recognized the importance of the mind-body connection and the power of spirituality to heal. Hippocrates and Plato in ancient Greece also recognized the importance of non-physical factors in healing and clearly acknowledged the significance of the doctor/patient relationship (Pappas S, Perlman A, 2002). The fields of religion, spirituality, and medicine were intertwined in most ancient cultures throughout the world – even in cultures and peoples that otherwise had very different beliefs, customs, and lifestyles and were located in distant parts of the world.

Integrity is essential to a compassionate, trusting and lasting doctor/patient relationship. In contrast to the current time, there were periods throughout history when physicians were not completely truthful with their patients. In fact, physicians in some instances specifically withheld information or intentionally deceived their patients of reports of a virulent or deadly disease. Why was this done? It was felt, particularly when limited or no effective therapies were available, that the patient's knowledge of having an aggressive or deadly disease would more rapidly lead to his deterioration or death. Again, this practice indicates the widespread belief throughout history of a strong mind-body connection and the power of the mind to effect one's physical health. Physicians rationalized this deceptive behavior as a mechanism to prevent or reduce pain, suffering, and even death by their patients. In recent times, the Universal Declaration of Human Rights Act by the General Assembly of the United Nations in 1948 established a new standard of care (General Assembly of the United Nations, 1948). This Act was based on the Universal Doctrine of human dignity and ethics – it is no longer acceptable to withhold medical reports and truth from the patient. Truthfulness and integrity are essential human rights and ethics has assumed primary importance in the practice of clinical medicine.

Cancer therapy requires the most powerful and toxic treatments known to man. Cancer surgeons, such as Dr. Michael Torosian, are often the first physicians to diagnose and treat the cancer patient. The initial cancer treatment is clearly a time of critical importance and sets the stage for all future events for that patient. When the cancer can be surgically removed, a sense of victory over this formidable disease surfaces for the first time since its diagnosis. The news of successful surgery is clearly a welcome relief and gives hope for recovery and cure to the patient and his family. Along with this sense of victory and optimism, however, is a feeling of cautious restraint. Other treatments, including chemotherapy and radiation therapy, are often needed in the months ahead. Additional testing may be required to determine if the tumor has spread to other parts of the body. Finally, despite all of our current treatments and high tech studies, one is always aware that the tumor can recur.

Great compassion must be exhibited by the physician at this time. He must understand not only the physical but also the emotional, psychologic, and spiritual trauma experienced by the cancer patient. Empathy, integrity, truthfulness, and honesty form the cornerstone of a strong and trusting doctor/patient relationship and are essential qualities of the very best oncologic physicians. The physician must communicate with his patient in an accurate, understandable and sensitive way – with utmost compassion and care. The patient should never need to doubt the accuracy of the information provided by his physician and must be able to approach his physician to question any uncertainties or gaps in the information provided. Many questions arise during this period of anxiety, fear, and uncertainty experienced by the patient newly diagnosed with cancer. Compassion, faith and hope expressed during this critical time can play a significant role in the process of healing and recovery. The cancer diagnosis is life-changing and is one of the greatest physical and spiritual challenges a person can face. This difficult and complex challenge can strengthen or destroy one's spiritual and emotional essence. However, no one needs to suffer from the emotional or spiritual trauma of cancer – we will show you how to confront this challenge to achieve personal growth and to attain complete spiritual healing.

Truly great cancer physicians can facilitate the healing process by their words, their actions and their own spirit during this critical time. The sensitivity and empathy exhibited by one's physician is as important as providing accurate medical information and providing appropriate medical care. God and the power of spirituality are great sources of strength and comfort for patients and physicians alike. When God is invited into the process of healing, one can endure illness and continue living life to its greatest potential. Prayer places the patient and the doctor in a position of power, a power beyond medical knowledge and skill. The patient can be empowered to live without fear and with hope for the future. Spiritual healing can facilitate recovery from many illnesses but assumes particular importance here because of the tremendous emotional and psychologic impact of cancer.

Supporting the importance of compassion and spirituality in healing is a provocative essay published by Engel 25 years ago lamenting the state of medicine at that time (Engel GL, 1977). The content of his report remains relevant today and demonstrated that medicine suffered from defining disease and health solely by physical parameters. Physical or biologic factors defined illness and disease – therefore, physical and biologic therapies predominated the treatment approach. Psychosocial issues clearly resided outside the scope of medicine at that time and Engel emphatically stated that excluding these critical, non-biologic factors was creating a crisis in the practice of medicine. He reiterated the importance of the mind-body connection recognized by ancient physicians thousands of years earlier. Specifically, Engel hypothesized that biologic, psychologic, and social factors needed to be considered to properly define and treat disease. The ancient concept and significance of the mind-body connection in the genesis and treatment of human disease was being revived. The power of spirituality is now clearly evident and can empower the cancer patient to attain complete spiritual healing.

Great physicians throughout history have consistently exemplified respect and sincere compassion for their patients. Sir William Osler (1849 - 1919) is commonly regarded as the Father of Modern Medicine (MacLeod R, 2001). Osler taught and practiced medicine with a very humanistic, warm, and common sense approach. He was revered as a great and compassionate physician by his patients and internationally renowned to the medical community as an extraordinary clinician-educator. The doctor/patient relationship was of paramount importance to Osler and respect for the patient was an important virtue of his medical practice. Osler's principles and teachings have continued to influence the academic and clinical practice of medicine to the current time.

Communication between the patient and his physician is critically important to achieving a trusting, effective doctor/patient relationship. Truthfulness and accuracy are integral components of every communication between a physician and his patient. The patient should never need to doubt the accuracy of information provided by his physician and must be able to approach his physician to question any uncertainties or gaps in the knowledge of his disease. The physician's medical knowledge must be current, clear, and relevant to his patient's clinical situation. The physician should instill confidence in the patient and must never exhibit an arrogant or condescending manner, the latter being all too common in the medical profession today.

During medical training, physicians are taught to achieve excellence in the intellectual and technical aspects of medicine – providing an accurate diagnosis, formulating the most appropriate treatment plan, and remaining current on the latest clinical trials and research. But, the technical aspects of medicine frequently prevent the development of an effective doctor-patient relationship. What about the humanistic side of medicine? Needed skills include communicating, listening, relating to a patient in crisis, sensing a patient's response to this terrifying diagnosis, being aware of the patient's need for reassurance and trust, exhibiting confidence and competency, and, most of all, being compassionate during this critical stage of a patient's life.

A physician must learn to communicate his medical knowledge with effective interpersonal skills – every meeting between a physician and his patient should be considered an opportunity to exhibit compassion. Compassion, warmth, and understanding from the patient's perspective are essential to developing an effective doctor/patient relationship. Physicians must show understanding of the cancer diagnosis from the patient's perspective to truly connect with him. The patient must be considered an equal and treated with complete respect by the physician at all times. In other words, the patient's fears, concerns, and expectations must be heard and effectively managed. Patients have unique concerns, questions, and challenges when confronted with the diagnosis of cancer and these issues must be constructively and compassionately met. Physicians, especially surgeons, are typically taught to put their emotions and feelings aside in order to more objectively provide treatment. However, surgeons and all physicians must realize that complete healing of any illness, particularly one as difficult as cancer, requires warmth, understanding and compassion needed to connect with another human being.

Communication between the doctor and his patient must be completely open – that is, all interactions must be a two-way dialogue, not an instructive lesson taught by the physician. Listening to the patient is essential to making this connection and will allow the communication to focus on areas of particular interest and concern to the patient. Most cancer patients today are facing multiple types of therapy, including surgery, chemotherapy, and radiation therapy. Besides the personal challenge of undergoing and recovering from these treatments, patient concerns extend to their family, friends, co-workers, and their entire social network. The emotional and psychologic impact of cancer and its treatments create an enormous burden for each patient. Some of these burdens are unique to each patient, being dependent upon the particular physical, social and professional circumstances involved. Nevertheless, each and every concern is important and significant to that patient and must be viewed that way.

Physicians must recognize that each patient has a unique personality, a unique set of social circumstances and a unique spirituality. It is imperative that the physician recognize the uniqueness of his individual patients and their differing thoughts, concerns, and challenges. Time continuously marches on and presents each of us with new challenges, problems, and opportunities. Our personal, social, professional, and medical conditions are constantly changing. A physician must not be totally consumed with the medical or physical illness of his patients at the exclusion of the personal, social, professional and spiritual aspects of their lives. To do so would be to ignore the world in which his patient lives – and to ignore the emotional, psychologic and spiritual components of his illness. Complete healing requires that conventional medical therapy by placed in the context of this larger picture, since these other worlds are also constantly changing and influencing one's physical health. Our goal is to achieve healing of the spirit, which clearly interacts with each of these other worlds of existence.

Different cancer patients want to know variable amounts of information. Some patients today want to know as many details as possible about their particular cancer – for example, the cell type, the proliferation index, the growth fraction, hormone receptor analysis, all aspects of clinical and pathologic staging, and the status of specific oncogene markers. There is a tremendous amount of information available from pathologic and genetic analysis of tumor cells with current technology. Similarly, there is a wealth of information on the Internet and patients frequently use this source to gain more detailed knowledge about their cancer. Some of the information on the Internet is accurate and some is not. However, it is all accessible to the patient, their families and the general public. The physician must be available to help patients interpret this information and to focus the patient's attention on material that is relevant to his condition. This will avoid unnecessary and often counter-productive gathering of irrelevant, misleading, or inaccurate information by the patient. Cancer is complex enough without confusing the issue with information overload or, even worse, mis-information.

Doctors must provide ample time for patients and their families to ask probing and important questions about this difficult disease – and patients must feel extremely comfortable doing so. The response to these questions often affects the everyday lives of cancer patients in a very real and personal way. Physicians must take this responsibility seriously and realize the impact that their words have on their patients' lives. Physicians cannot be abrupt, curt, demeaning or insensitive to patient or family concerns. Respect of and for the patient is one of the cornerstones of developing an effective doctor/patient relationship. It may take weeks, months, or even years to establish a trusting, supportive doctor/patient relationship, but the converse is not true – the connecting bond between a physician and his patient can be destroyed in seconds with a few unkind, insincere, or thoughtless words.

Klein and his colleagues conducted a randomized study of medical students in the United Kingdom to assess interviewing skills (Klein S, Tracy D, Kitchener HC, Walker LG, 2000). This study demonstrated the importance of listening to patients with cancer. Although this conclusion may seem self-evident, it must be put into practice by the medical community at large. It was found that students who interviewed cancer patients demonstrated increased empathy and trust, an improved ability to listen, and enhanced assessment of symptoms. Medical students interviewing patients without cancer demonstrated decreased abilities in each of these areas. Thus, interacting with cancer patients has unique challenges and difficulties, but, also presents specific opportunities and benefits for the compassionate and receptive physician. It is not only the cancer patient who has the opportunity to grow, to learn and to transform spiritually during this journey. The understanding and perceptive physician must always be open to learning from his patients – the authors of this compelling book are two such physicians who constantly grow and strive to improve their skills to help their patients deal with many aspects of cancer.

The physician must remain optimistic without providing false hope to the patient or his family. For example, with a 75%

chance of cure for a particular patient, the healing physician would express optimism, provide hope and develop an effective treatment plan for cure. Alternatively, a negative and callous approach would emphasize the 25% chance of failure – waiting and almost expecting the cancer to recur. This approach is unfair, unnecessary and would naturally promote fear and anxiety. The pessimistic approach is all too common in the medical profession and can be very detrimental to the patient's physical and spiritual well being. In contrast, the healing approach would clearly indicate that the goal of treatment is cure – in fact, cure is three times more likely to occur in this scenario as tumor recurrence. Fear and anxiety can and should be avoided. Faith, hope, and compassion would create an atmosphere which facilitates treatment success and complete healing – including the physical, emotional, psychologic and spiritual aspects of one's life.

Devising a plan of action and providing hope for the cancer patient are critically important. In the best situations, a treatment regimen which is highly effective against the tumor can be prescribed – this treatment plan may include surgery, radiation therapy, chemotherapy or any combination of these therapies. In some instances, clinical trials are used as a means to provide the best and latest treatment options. However, sometimes cure is not possible and relief of symptoms is the goal of therapy – a treatment plan to provide relief and to improve quality of life is then pursued. Providing hope, faith and support is an essential component of every treatment plan. Hope and faith can strengthen one's spirit during difficult times. Without hope, despair, depression, frustration and anger can set in. Cancer must be confronted on all levels, including the physical, emotional, psychological and spiritual levels, in order to be to defeated.

Cancer is unpredictable, not only for the patient, but also

for the physician. It is important for the physician <u>not</u> to give dogmatic predictions of outcome. Particularly inaccurate are estimates of survival. Now, there are some generalizations that can be made based on tumor type, stage of disease, growth rates of tumor cells and other specific information that can be shared with the patient. However, many intangible factors exist that can dramatically alter patient outcome – not the least of which is the topic of this book, the power of spirituality. Spirituality has tremendous health benefits for a wide range of diseases, including cardiovascular, neurologic, psychologic, and immunologic diseases as well as cancer. The beneficial effects of spirituality and religion have been documented by scientific study in the medical literature. Undoubtedly, studies will continue to be published to demonstrate the incredible phenomenon of spiritual healing, and pioneering research is actively being conducted in this area. Spirituality has the capacity to improve recovery from surgery, to reduce side effects of therapy, to improve quality of life, and to offer hope, serenity, and peacefulness when other resources have been exhausted. These effects have tremendous potential to benefit cancer patients at all stages of their disease or treatment regimen.

Patients must always be treated with utmost respect and human dignity. Their physicians must exhibit professionalism and the highest ethical conduct possible at all times. However, in today's healthcare environment, there are practical and economic obstacles to developing the warm and compassionate doctor/patient relationship we have been discussing. Current economic pressures encourage physicians to practice high volume medicine with short office visits, leaving limited time for effective communication. Today's physicians are more specialized and tend to rely on high tech testing as opposed to bedside diagnosis. Internet access by patients and physicians alike depersonalizes medical interaction and further distances the patient from his doctor. In the final analysis, the diseased part of the body becomes our focus of attention – that is, the disease becomes magnified out of proportion to the rest of individual. This distortion impairs the doctor/patient relationship and depersonalizes our human essence. Distorting and depersonalizing the human image impairs our healing of the whole person. Spirituality has the capacity and breadth of power to maintain perspective and to achieve complete healing of the cancer patient.

When possible, it is beneficial to give some control back to the patient and his family. For example, many decisions along the journey to healing involve a choice between several options. When treatment options are equivalent, patients should be aware that alternatives exist and should be encouraged to actively participate in selecting the most appropriate treatment plan. For example, treatment of early stage prostate cancer can be accomplished with equal rates of success by surgery or radiation therapy. Men with this disease must be knowledgeable of both treatment options in order to make a truly informed treatment decision. Recovery from surgery is significant and may be complicated by impotence and voiding problems. Alternatively, radiation therapy can cause significant local irritation and inflammation of the pelvis, causing long-term cystitis and proctitis. The risks and benefits of these treatment approaches must be thoroughly explained when appropriate and an elective, uncoerced decision be made by the patient. No one treatment plan is right for everyone with prostate cancer or any other type of cancer.

Patients faced with the stress and anxiety of cancer

commonly present with physical symptoms. Disbelief, denial, difficulty in making decisions, fear, hopelessness, anxiety, sadness, anger, irritability, and depression can result from the diagnosis of cancer. Further fear can be evoked if the symptoms are ignored or disregarded as unimportant. One of our patients complained of dizziness, blurred vision, headaches and tremors – although he feared it was his cancer that had spread, his symptoms were caused by intense anxiety and fear. A vicious cycle was created – the more he dwelled on his fearful thoughts, the stronger and more intense his symptoms became. With each phase of cancer survivorship, there are different stressors that will continue to challenge one's coping ability. Every routine medical visit, x-ray, blood test, change in physical appearance, pain, weakness, fatigue, and tiredness are a reminder of one's vulnerability.

Fear is one of our most constricting and debilitating emotions, causing feelings ranging from uneasiness to complete insecurity. Intense fear limits our perceptions, our thoughts, and our physical actions. However, fear is not always based on a realistic threat. In fact, the simplest and most effective explanation of fear was conveyed to me by one of my college professors with the acronym as follows:

F = False

E = Evidence

A = Appear

R = Real

I have worked with cancer patients for many years and have often needed to treat emotional injury and needless trauma inflicted on them by an insensitive physician. Even the strongest and most compassionate doctor/patient relationship can be destroyed in seconds by a thoughtless remark, negating months or even years of hard work. For example, Maura is a 43-year-old ovarian cancer patient who came to therapy for intense anxiety and fear after learning her diagnosis. She worked hard to get over these feelings and after months of therapy, she was finally able to sleep and begin to enjoy her family. One visit to her medical oncologist destroyed everything. Her oncologist suggested another cycle of chemotherapy and Maura asked if this type of treatment would cause her to gain weight. While still looking down into Maura's chart, the oncologist frowned and responded "Your tumor is growing larger and you worry about weight gain?" Maura was speechless and was too shocked to respond. She called me from a pay phone at the medical center and immediately came to my office shaking and trembling, numb with fear. She lost the trust and respect in her doctor that had been established over the past 6 months and she instantly reverted to her world of fear and anxiety. She changed physicians, eventually established a trusting relationship with a new doctor, and elected to have further chemotherapy. This incident occurred 6 years ago and Maura is now doing well.

Cancer patients are particularly attentive to each and every word spoken by their physician. Especially at critical points in their clinical course, remarks and comments made by their physician are almost engraved into their minds. Consider the case of Molly, a 37-year-old nurse with cancer, who was managing her life and coping with her disease as well as she possibly could. On a routine visit, she asked her oncologist about the possibility of a recurrence. The oncologist replied it was just a matter of time, but she should not lose sleep worrying about it. Molly was stunned and tried to ask more questions – but her oncologist had no more time to spend with her that day. She was emotionally devastated and told that she had an overactive imagination and to see a psychiatrist. This comment re-played over and over again in Molly's mind like a tape recorder – this occurred for one month until she was finally convinced that she needed help. The only thing that Molly heard from her physician that day was that the cancer will come back and that it was only a matter of time. But, how much time? This fear triggered questions and uncertainties and her logical conclusion was "When am I going to die?" She became helpless, lost hope for recovery and sank into a deep depression for two months. All of this unnecessary fear, anxiety and depression could have been avoided if compassion and sensitivity had been displayed by her physician.

Hopelessness is a symptom of depression and anxiety. Many times during the course of an illness such as cancer, hope seems remote. The comfort and security of hope can slip through our hands like the grains of fine sand. One of the most important contributions a doctor can make to the care of his patients is hope – no situation is entirely hopeless since the future cannot be accurately predicted. It is true. Despite all of our current technology, oncologists cannot precisely predict clinical outcome. There are too many complex variables to consider.

When depressed, we often confuse feelings and fears with facts. Our feelings of hopelessness and despair are symptoms of depression and may not be based in reality. The conviction of hopelessness is one of the most characteristic and devastating aspects of depression. In fact, the degree of hopelessness experienced by seriously depressed patients with an excellent prognosis can be markedly greater than that seen in non-depressed, terminal cancer patients. By eliminating depression from the cancer patient, quality of life can be dramatically improved. Emotional suffering is commonly caused by a negative attitude and rarely by a malignant tumor – anger, despair, and hopelessness must be avoided. These feelings can be as destructive as the cancer itself and can inhibit one's progress along the journey to emotional and spiritual healing. Understanding our spiritual existence and knowing that there is more to this life than our biological and physical existence empowers our soul.

Spiritual healing demands more than science – it requires encouraging the patient to be hopeful, to expect a positive outcome and to have faith and hope in God. A physician who communicates with a heartfelt simplicity is inspiring and moving to his patients. To treat patients with compassion, honesty, respect and a gentle graciousness promotes complete healing. A physician's true effectiveness lies in his ability to give of himself, his devotion, his love and his compassion and to realize that he is anointed by God to care for His people. Illness is not a punishment from God – if so, why would we return to Him so often for healing. God is love and creates love – healing happens when we begin to love. Our human spirit is stronger than our body and mind and will survive beyond our physical existence. But, sometimes our human heart becomes hardened and our feelings are shut down. God then needs to gently piece our heart back together so that we can open ourselves to the love and tenderness around us. The Jewish Old Testament referred to this as a "circumcision of the heart" – today's vernacular might call this "spiritual open heart surgery." Healing can only be achieved when we begin to open our hearts to love, to have compassion, and to release our angry and hostile feelings.

Physicians as well as patients must have an open and receptive spirit – giving and receiving goes both ways in the relationship between doctor and patient. I will never forget

Willis, a 64-year-old man who lived in one of the poorest urban neighborhoods. Willis was a medical miracle, his medical history was as long as I had ever seen. He was diabetic and had survived prostate cancer, colon cancer, heart bypass surgery, several strokes and many other medical problems. Willis presented with severe chest pain, which fortunately was not related to further heart trouble but was due to anxiety. He suffered for years from debilitating depression and sadness and had no surviving family. You could not help but love Willis – he was tall in stature but conveyed a childlike innocence and looked at the world through a pair of big brown eyes. He looked remarkably groomed, notwithstanding the ordeal of years of recurrent hospitalizations with major surgery, marked by numerous complications, including several strokes. He was so depressed that he stayed in bed all day without talking to anyone. He told me that he always enjoyed going to church but that he could not even do that anymore. Willis was loved in his neighborhood and was thankful that he was able to work until his retirement at age 60. I told Willis that I was determined to see that sparkle back in his big brown eyes and he smiled and said, "That's all I want, that sparkle back." I then called his pastor and asked him to schedule visits with Willis and his friends from church. Every day friends came to joke with him, pray with him and talk about old times. Willis then improved, got out of bed and started going to church by himself. One day he came to my office for his appointment and as he walked in, he pointed to the eyes I learned to love so much and said, "See that, see that sparkle?" In fact, there was a glow in Willis I had not seen before. At the end of our session, he asked me if he could say a prayer for me. He gently took my hands and surrounded them with his strong hands and began to pray. His words were powerful and his voice authoritative, almost demanding, telling God to take care of me and asking Him to protect me. Willis' eyes filled with tears. I felt empowered and deeply touched by his words, his prayer and his strength. No one had ever prayed with me that way that I was surprised how much energy and faith Willis possessed – I did not know that he prayed his goodbye to me. That was the last time I saw Willis who died peacefully and happy, surrounded by his friends and neighbors at home. Willis has given me more than I could have ever given to him. I now think of Willis often and I thank him. Somehow I feel that he is still praying for me. No textbook knowledge equals what I learned from Willis, who allowed me to look into his eyes and into his soul. My most precious memories are of patients facing nearly impossible challenges with faith and courage – an enduring friendship and a lasting bond can be established at those times that reach beyond the boundary of death. Such experiences have spiritually expanded my limits and, as was once told to me, "Once we are truly stretched, we never return to our former dimension."

The power of a doctor's compassion and loving care can gently bring a cancer patient to the heart of God and God's universe. The spiritual journey is a lifelong trek that deeply affects our relationship with others. Each step we take toward understanding ourselves brings us closer to those with whom we share our lives. One of the greatest gifts that one's doctor can bestow at times like this is communication with his heart and teaching that there is nothing to fear, not even death. There is no death for our spiritual existence – our spirit is eternal.

The caring and compassionate physician is essential to prevent deterioration of one's spirit and soul by cancer. The best physicians understand and even anticipate the emotional and psychologic burdens which are so intrusive and harmful to the cancer patient. Physicians must be a source of unending compassion, warmth, generosity, hope, faith and love to their patients. Complete healing can only occur if the physical, emotional, psychologic, and spiritual needs of the cancer patient are fulfilled along with conventional medical therapy in a comprehensive treatment plan.

Our spiritual journey provides us with the opportunity for tremendous personal growth and spiritual transformation – both are needed to achieve complete healing. The power and strength of our spirit is unlimited – not even cancer can destroy the human spirit! We will show you how to strengthen and transform your spirit along this challenging journey. You can discover deep within your soul the **"spirit to heal!"**

CHAPTER 3

THE WORLDS OF SCIENCE AND SPIRITUALITY CLASH

"Science without religion is lame,
religion without science is blind."

Albert Einstein (1879 -1952)

Over 100,000 years ago, our prehistoric ancestors used rituals when burying the dead. In fact, nearly every human culture has used a form of religion or prayer during periods of stress, disease and health. Since the beginning of recorded history, healing of disease and illness was closely connected to the religious beliefs of human culture – despite the fact that some of these ancient cultures were located on opposite sides of the earth. Remember, there were no telephones or television or e-mail to connect these different peoples – and there was no common language to allow verbal communication. Yet, a common theme in these ancient cultures was the intimate connection between medicine and religion.

Early doctors in Greece and Egypt were thought to borrow their powers from true gods in order to heal the sick (Porter R, 1997). The Greek Aesculapius and the Egyptian Imhotep (ca. 3500 B.C.) were mortals who were later elevated to the level of gods in the field of medicine. Greek temples were erected to Aesculapius and the sick and diseased would come to these temples to be healed. They would pray, present a sacrifice to the gods, and then sleep – it is believed that, in their dreams, physicians of that time would reveal how to heal their illness.

In early Greek society, there were two classes of physicians: priest-like physicians and physician-craftsmen (Carmichael AG, Ratzan RM, 1991). The priest-like physicians derived their powers from the gods and followed the teachings of Aesculapius. These physicians were scholarly and treated the elite of ancient Greece. The more practical and everyday aspects of healthcare were left to the physician-craftsmen. These latter physicians followed the Hippocratic school of disease and healing – this school developed theories of disease and very useful, practical therapies of cure. Hippocrates (ca. 400 B.C.), the father of Greek medicine, began to change the relationship which had existed between medicine and religion for thousands and thousands of years – that is, diseases and illness had physical causes with characteristic symptoms and specific, objective cures (Grmek MD, 1991). Sickness and health of mortal men were not just left to the will of the gods. Galen (ca 130-210 A.D.) lived 500 years after Hippocrates and synthesized the medical works of Hippocrates, the biologic findings of Aristotle and the philosophy of Plato. This enormous academic and practical work created a system of medical theory and practice that dominated Western medicine until the 19th century (Magner LN, 1992).

Ancient Egypt had an advanced system of medical diagnosis and treatment conducted by physician-priests. In fact, there were elaborate medical Papyri discovered in Egypt which described in detail theories of illness and aging, systematic diagnostic examinations and specific treatments for various medical conditions (Reeves C, 1992). The Ebers Papyrus (ca 1500 B.C.) predated Hippocrates by about 1000 years and contained practical treatments and remedies which drew upon even older sources of Egyptian medical works. The first operation ever depicted pictorally is circumcision, a procedure considered a religious rite and performed by an Egyptian physician-priest. This procedure was discovered on a wall carving in a Dynasty VI tomb and was created over 4000 years ago.

Other ancient cultures independently developed strong connections between medicine and religion – many of these cultures were separated by vast mountain ranges, deserts and oceans and, yet, individually devised theories of health and disease around their religious beliefs. Eastern medicine in India and China was closely interwoven with religion and spirituality – and those associations persist today. The body, mind and spirit exist in harmonic balance when healthy. An imbalance or disequilibrium in any of these components causes illness and disease. Equilibrium must be restored to successfully treat disease and restore health to the body. Modern Eastern medicine includes therapy with medicine and surgery but also prescribes dietary and lifestyle changes, exercises, massage, meditation and other means to treat the mind, body and spirit (Baker IA, 1997). In a completely separate culture, native American Indians developed their entire field of medical practice around religion and charms (Carmichael AG, Ratzan RM,1991). In fact, the word "medicine" means "mystery" when translated from their tribal languages – the practitioner of medicine was the "medicine-man" or "mystery-man." The medicine-man used remedies including roots and herbs, but also dealt with mysteries and charms. Such mysteries included donning a strange dress, dancing over the patient, singing songs and shaking rattles in hopes of evoking a cure with charms. If the disease was not cured and death occurred, it was the will of the Great Spirit. It is amazing that all of these ancient cultures shared this common bond between medicine and religion – or is it? Is it an instinct as primordial as the need for food, water or love? How else can one explain the deep-rooted connection between medicine and religion from ancient cultures scattered and separated across the vast expanse of our world?

Contrary to popular belief, medicine progressed in medieval times – even through the Dark Ages. Within the European continent, French cathedral schools offered superb medical training to clergy and layman – again, the connection between medicine and religion persisted (Kiple KF,1993). Medieval texts of medical works were extensive and went well beyond the scope of the Hippocratic oath. Besides practical and medical information on the diagnosis and treatment of disease, the spiritual importance of ethical medical practice was emphasized. At least for the field of medicine, it seems that the Dark Ages weren't so dark after all.

But soon, a cataclysmic clash was to occur between the worlds of science and religion. Hippocrates in ancient Greece only hinted at the practical, scientific side of medicine, which was clearly separate from the will or power of gods to effect healing or cause disease. Science was soon to challenge religion on all fronts – astronomy, physics, biology, and even medicine. Religious leaders viewed these scientific and intellectual challenges as heresy – these new beliefs conflicted with religious doctrines which had existed for hundreds or thousands of years. The Renaissance had begun!

Perhaps the most significant event which embodied the conflict between science and religion at that time was the prosecution of Galileo by the Catholic Church in 1633 for believing in the Copernican theory of the universe (Webster C, 1975). Nicholas Copernicus (1473-1543) postulated a new theory of the universe which correctly placed the Sun (not the Earth) at the center of our solar system. Until that time, it was widely held by church and state alike that the Earth was the center of the universe. The church had always believed in the cosmos with Earth and, therefore, mankind at the center of God's creation – this cosmologic theory was based on theories and observations previously made by Aristotle and Ptolemy. The universe was literally turned upside down by Copernicus' new celestial model placing Earth in planetary motion around the Sun. Because of strong opposition from the Catholic Church, Copernicus did not publish his theory until 1543, the year he died. His book "On the Revolution of the Celestial Spheres" revolutionized man's view of the universe – and of mankind itself. Copernicus, however, made one critical mistake in assuming that the planets orbited the sun in perfect circles, requiring him to make convoluted modifications to his celestial model – this ancient idea of circular planetary orbit proved to be incorrect. Johanne Kepler (1571-1630), a brilliant mathematician, theorized that planetary orbits were elliptical, not circular, and corrected this flaw in Copernicus' model.

Although Copernicus was cautious in revealing his revolutionary celestial theory, Galileo (1564-1642) openly championed the Copernican view of the universe. Galileo supported his belief in the Copernican model of the universe with scientific observations obtained with the latest technology of the time – the telescope. Galileo's observations through the telescope clearly ended the era of the Aristotelian-Ptolemic cosmos – the Earth could no longer be positioned at the center of the universe. This concept was simply untenable by the Catholic Church – it changed humanity forever. The Catholic Church realized the significance of this concept and the impending challenge from the scientific community to its authority – science was no longer constrained by rigid doctrines imposed by the church. When Galileo was prosecuted by the Catholic Church in 1633, he renounced his beliefs. But, the scientific revolution had begun and could not be subdued.

Scientific discovery occurred at a tremendous pace in the Renaissance and beyond. Roger Bacon (1219-1292) was a Franciscan priest who studied mathematics, music and astronomy and contributed greatly to the knowledge of the time (Suplee C, 2000). Despite his strong religious convictions, he recognized the importance of experimentation and observations in understanding science! He had to pursue much of his scientific work and writings in secrecy because of known opposition from his religious superiors. Certainly his greatest contribution was postulating the 4 steps of the scientific method – the basis of all scientific experimentation even today. The scientific method consists of making observations, generating a hypothesis or theory, predicting outcome based on that theory, and testing its validity by scientific experiments. In other words, science was no longer content to blindly follow beliefs or edicts which could not be proven – even those most fervently held by religious leaders. A great chasm had been created between science, including medicine, and religion.

Great progress in medicine, literature, art and architecture occurred throughout the Renaissance. In Greek and Roman antiquity, human anatomy was studied sparingly as very few physicians were permitted to perform anatomic dissection. In contrast, the human body was celebrated during the Renaissance, leading to rapid advancement in the understanding of human anatomy. The Venetian surgeon, Allessandro Bennedetti (ca. 1450-1512), and the Belgian surgeon and anatomist, Andreas Vesalius (1514-1564), published extensive, illustrated works of human anatomy (Wear A, French R, Loine I, 1985). Human anatomy was artistically and accurately depicted in comprehensive texts of that era. The Vatican did not officially approve dissection of corpses until 1537. Shortly thereafter, William Harvey (1578-1657) demonstrated that blood circulated throughout the body and was pumped by the heart – a radical concept in the year 1628 and one that challenged Galen's theory of blood proposed 1400 years earlier.

Scholars, academicians, and scientists have continued to challenge ancient dogma since that time. Remarkable scientific advances have been made throughout the Industrial Age and the Technology Boom. Scientific research and discovery occurs at a pace today which is unprecedented in the history of mankind. Furthermore, computer technology with satellite relay communications allows current discoveries to be dispersed worldwide instantaneously. Science has clearly diverged from religion. Is it time for these two worlds to re-unite?

Spirituality and medicine have become more integrated in recent years and should be considered complementary, not conflicting, methods of healing. Both patient and physician sentiments toward spirituality are evolving as its importance and relevance to medical practice is again being realized. Numerous studies exist to document the rebirth of this perception. In a 1992 poll, 93% of physicians believed that they should consider their patients' religious needs – yet, only 17% of these same physicians admitted to having significant religious discussions with their patients (King DE, Sobel J, Haggerty J et al, 1992). Another study of over 200 patients showed that 48% wanted their physicians to pray with them (King DE, Bushwick B, 1994). However, it is rare for patients to openly express that desire. Why does this dichotomy exist between spiritual wants and medical practice? In my 16 years of practicing cancer surgery, only one patient has asked me to pray with her, just before starting surgery. We both prayed at that time and surgery went well – but, so many other patients must have similar desires which simply go unspoken. One of the most striking findings comes from a 1996 poll of 296 family physicians – a remarkable 99% of these physicians believed that religious faith could heal (Sloan RP, Bagiella, E, Powell T, 1999). Evidence now exists to support this widespread belief!

Several hundred clinical studies have now been performed to determine the effect of spirituality on health outcome. The vast majority of these studies show a positive relationship between spirituality and improved medical outcome. Spirituality and attendance at religious services are associated with reduction of stress, recovery from illness and surgery, reduction of depression and pain, improved control of blood pressure and coronary artery disease, and recovery from substance abuse (Mueller PS, Plevak DJ, Rummans TA, 2001). In cancer patients, studies have consistently shown that spirituality and religion help patients cope with the emotional consequences of their illness – in fact, those with the highest level of spirituality seem to experience the lowest level of anxiety (Kaczorowski JM, 1989). Some reports even show that spirituality can be associated with improved immunity in cancer patients, possibly preventing infection or even combating cancer cells (Sephton SE, Koopman C, Schaal M et al, 2001).

How does spirituality influence one's health? Is there a direct or indirect link between spirituality and health – or the absence of spirituality and illness? Are there specific, physiologic effects which occur during prayer, meditation and other forms of religious practice to account for the observed medical benefits? The answers to these critical questions remain unknown. Certainly spirituality strengthens one's social network, reduces anxiety, stress, and depression, and may improve one's immune system. Undoubtedly, the effects of spirituality on one's health are complex, multifactorial and somewhat mysterious when compared to the precise, more tangible laws and forces which govern our physical universe.

Every person has a unique spirituality – like one's personality, fingerprint pattern or genetic constitution. Spirituality and religion are distinct entities – although spirituality includes one's religion, it is far more complex and mysterious than that. Spirituality embodies faith in a Greater Power, trust, hope, prayer, meditation, enhanced coping skills, personal transcendence, and one's ultimate purpose in life. Spirituality is flexible, personal and represents the functional or dynamic aspects of life. In contrast, religion is much more structured, rigid and adherent to doctrine. Religion refers to an institutional, as opposed to an individual, set of beliefs which is less open to interpretation. Spirituality and religion are complex phenomena and can affect us in many, many different ways.

The existence and nature of the human spirit and soul have been the subject of philosophic and theologic debates for thousands of years. Aristotle regarded the soul as critically important in maintaining good, physical health. The import of the mind-body connection was evident in the writings and teachings of this ancient Greek scholar (Grmek MD, 1991). Our spirit can transcend the intellectual capacity of our mind to reason and can sense feelings beyond the limits of our physical being.

We believe the primary function of the human spirit is to communicate with God and others on another, higher level – our spirit has innate wisdom and energy that reaches out to others. The human spirit works in mystical, mysterious, and wonderous ways and nurtures us with love, hope, faith, serenity and the power to heal.

The soul, we believe, represents the structure of our character and personality. Our spirit lives in, through, and beyond our soul – our spirit represents our true, inner core. Our soul represents the fabric, or clothing, of the spirit. A "lost soul" is one who has lost his connection to God – has lost his way on the spiritual journey of personal transformation. He must then find his way back on the pathway to God to achieve peace, love and the spirit to heal. The mind and spirit interact in an intricate and complex manner. We are, however, beginning to crack this code and obtain some insight into the workings of the human mind and spirit.

It is somewhat ironic that science has recently come back to religion – not to blindly accept its doctrines, but to scientifically investigate the nature of religious experiences, such as prayer and meditation. Can the biology of belief be objectively studied? Do measurable, physiologic changes occur in our brains during prayer, meditation or mystic experiences? Do prayer and meditation evoke similar biologic changes in the brain? The fascinating answer to these questions is a resounding, "Yes."

Exciting research has been performed to investigate changes in brain function during meditation, prayer and other religious experiences. Early studies revealed changes in the electrical activity of the brain during meditation by Zen practitioners (Hirai T, 1974). Using electroencephalography (EEG), the electrical activity of the brain can be accurately mapped. Meditation was found to cause a significant change in electrical activity of the frontal lobe of the brain – the same area known to be involved in our emotional state. More recent studies using high-tech SPECT (single photon emission computed tomography) imaging has shown remarkable changes in brain activity with meditation and prayer (Newberg A, D'aquili E, Rause V, 2001). Newberg and D'Aquili used SPECT imaging to measure functional activity in different parts of the brain during religious experiences. SPECT activity is measured by radioactivity delivered to various parts of the brain based on blood flow. Increased blood flow correlates with increased brain activity and measurements can be obtained at the height of a deeply religious or spiritual experience. These investigators studied Buddhists during meditation and Franciscan nuns at prayer and found fascinating results. During meditation and prayer, similar changes in brain function were noted – increased activity was found in the left brain orientation association area (anatomically, the back, left side of the brain). Under normal conditions, this area of the brain helps to orient our physical body to the external world. Isn't it intriguing that, in deep states of meditation and prayer, "knowledge" of our physical orientation in space is reduced. Do these changes in brain function account for being at one with the universe for Buddhists in meditation and for closeness to God for sisters at prayer? Do spirituality and deep religious experiences result from specific, physiologic changes in brain function?

These philosophic, ethical and, to some extent, scientific questions remain unanswered. Spiritual, religious and mystical experiences may never be fully understood at the neurochemical level of brain biology. Remember the wisdom of native Americans whose medicine-man literally meant "mystery-man."

Some mysteries may never be completely solved or understood – not everything can be reduced to a mathematical equation or a biologic reaction. What is clear is that the worlds of science and spirituality need to re-unite to achieve even greater scientific and spiritual progress in the future. The Great Divide between these two worlds must vanish. We will now embark on a journey of spiritual transformation and discovery that could change your life forever!

CHAPTER 4

FEAR OF THE UNKNOWN

**"When I am with God
My fear is gone.
In the great quiet of God
My troubles are as the pebbles on the road,
My joys are like the everlasting hills."**

Walter Rauschenbusch (1861 - 1918)

Fear of the unknown is perhaps the most destructive and disheartening force to the human spirit. Why is this so? It is because fear permeates every thought, impulse, and action of our being. It insidiously invades the essence of the human soul – our mind, our willpower, and our spirit. Yes, fear attacks one's spirit like cancer invades one's body. Fear and cancer are parasites that thrive by robbing our mind and body of the essence of life. They are unwelcome intruders into our worlds, one spiritual and one physical. Yet, the human spirit and body are remarkable in their capacity to conquer these intruders and to restore serenity, peacefulness, and wellness to our being.

Cancer is the most feared diagnosis worldwide – feared because of its uncertainty and unpredictability. But, even before the diagnosis of cancer is established, fear begins when certain physical or x-ray findings raise the possibility that cancer is present. Even the slightest chance that cancer might exist can initiate a flood of tremendous emotional and psychologic turmoil. One can suddenly be taken from a state of peacefulness and serenity and be hurled into a world of mental and emotional chaos. The suddenness, coldness, and starkness of this crisis threatens one's mental and physical stability – immediate effects can challenge one's personal, family, social, professional, psychologic, and spiritual foundations. It is, indeed, a harsh reality check, which abruptly focuses one's attention on his well being and even survival. Everything else in life is suddenly put into perspective. One's mortality becomes clearly evident. Time seems to stand still.

Consider the 43-year-old woman with no breast symptoms who comes to see her physician for routine examination. Her yearly mammogram is performed and shows a new area of clustered calcifications in the breast for which biopsy is recommended. The mammogram indicates that the calcifications are probably benign, but the woman fears a diagnosis of cancer. She cannot sleep or eat normally until the biopsy is performed and wants to have surgery performed as soon as possible. Although she has never taken a sedative or anti-anxiety medication in the past, she calls her surgeon to request a prescription "to calm her nerves" the day before surgery. Surgical biopsy is performed and shows benign fibrocystic disease – her problems with anxiety, sleeping, and eating immediately resolve. Her fear is gone – her life quickly returns to normal.

Another example is a 61-year-old executive who has been a heavy smoker (two packs of cigarettes daily) for over 40 years. He develops a persistent cough and chest x-ray reveals an irregular nodule in the upper lobe of the left lung. His physician suspects cancer and recommends biopsy of the lung nodule. The executive has an important business trip in two weeks and plans to schedule the biopsy when he returns from that meeting. During the next two weeks, he continues to smoke two and sometimes three packs of cigarettes daily. He is anxious and works even longer and harder than usual. He does not discuss the results of his chest x-ray or the need for biopsy of this nodule with anyone, not even his wife of 37 years. He does not yet accept the possibility that he might have lung cancer and, especially, that its treatment might interfere with his work. His productivity is crucial to the success of his company. What will happen to the future of his company if he requires a lengthy medical absence to undergo treatment for lung cancer? No one has ever had to take his place in business negotiations in the past – in fact, he rarely took vacation and never missed more than a few days of work in a row. Who or how many people would be needed to take his place during his absence? His fear conjures up these questions that are repressed by the constant demand of his work. He elects to deny his health problem at this time and is literally consumed by his work. This type of reaction is common in career-oriented individuals, and particularly, but not exclusively, in men. Four weeks later he undergoes fine needle aspiration biopsy and the diagnosis of cancer is confirmed.

Uncertainty and fear dominate one's feelings and emotions when confronted with signs and symptoms suggesting the possibility of cancer. Even before the diagnosis of cancer is established, fear of this unknown but dreaded diagnosis can adversely impact one's physical, emotional and spiritual well-being. This fear can be devastating to even the strongest of individuals – it can be paralyzing to one's mental, physical, and spiritual state. Fear can cause panic, anxiety, depression, fatigue, hopelessness and many other physical and mental symptoms.

However, fear is not necessarily a bad emotional response. In fact, in some situations, it can be lifesaving. Fear is part of the "fight or flight" response, a basic human reaction that has been selected and preserved in the human genome over millions of years of evolution. The fight or flight response is man's physiologic reaction to startling, threatening or dangerous events. An instantaneous and highly regulated series of physiologic events occurs to prepare our body for action – to "fight" (i.e., to struggle or compete against our foe) or to "fly" (i.e., to run or remove our self from the threat). For instance, consider prehistoric man hunting in the woods for food – all of a sudden, a huge mountain lion appears in front of him. Our hunter's eyes become huge and fixed on the mountain lion, his heart races, his muscles become tense and pulsate as blood rushes to them, he sweats profusely, he is alert and mentally focused, all of his senses are keenly centered on the mountain lion. He is ready to "fight" his fierce competitor or take "flight" and run away. The "fight or flight" response is a survival instinct essential to saving one's life or, in the greater context, preserving the human race against its predators.

How does the "fight or flight" response work? This remarkable physiologic process is caused by an immediate and nearly complete stimulation of the neuroendocrine system (Guyton AC, Hall JE, 2000; Braunwald E, Hauser SL, Fauci AS, et al, 2001). Fear or fright activates a regulatory center in the brain called the hypothalamus. Stimulation of the hypothalamus in this way causes mass discharge of a portion of the nervous system called the sympathetic nerves. Mass discharge of the sympathetic nerves increases our ability to perform vigorous physical activity, such as "fight or flight". Sympathetic nerve stimulation also causes a rapid release of epinephrine and norepinephrine, two potent stimulating hormones from the adrenal gland. These stimulating hormones are released into the bloodstream and cause widespread effects throughout our body, preparing it for action.

The "fight or flight" response is one of the most dramatic and violent physiologic events that can occur in the human body. Global stimulation of organs and systems occurs throughout the body by one of two mechanisms: (1) direct stimulation by sympathetic nerve endings or (2) indirect chemical stimulation by the blood-borne adrenal hormones, epinephrine and norepinephrine (Braunwald E, Hauser SL, Fauci AS et al, 2001). Some of the effects caused by this physiologic response include: increased blood pressure and heart rate, increased blood flow to skeletal muscles, increased muscular strength, increased mental acuity and activity, increased metabolic rate, increased blood glucose levels, increased sweating and increased blood clotting ability (Guyton AC, Hall JE, 2000). Dramatic functional changes in our body occur within seconds of activating this response. The "fight or flight" response is short-lived – it must be as it wreaks havoc with the normal, resting state of our body. Mass discharge of the sympathetic nerves depletes our body of energy, exhausts our muscles, fatigues our mind, and imposes great physical demands on our heart and lungs. This response exists as a survival mechanism. Fear of immediate danger, as illustrated in our mountain lion story, is well-suited to this physiologic event. The challenge is imminent; the response, instantaneous; and the outcome, rapid.

Chronic fear, such as that experienced by cancer patients, is not the same. Mass discharge of the sympathetic nerves cannot be maintained for a prolonged time – the nerves tire and soon return to normal, baseline activity. Rapid depletion of the adrenal hormones prevents us from maintaining high hormone levels required for prolonged stimulation of our body. The "fight or flight" response is not designed for long-term use. Instead, chronic fear is destructive, debilitating and damaging to our body and psyche. Prolonged feelings of fear cause depression, hopelessness, anxiety, fatigue, irritability, weakness, anorexia, insomnia and many other physical and mental symptoms. Fear of this sort must be relieved so that our body, our mind and our spirit can live.

Let's again consider our patient, Sister Rose, and we will see that fear arises even in those with the strongest faith and spirituality. Her fear of cancer was compounded by the presence of a heart tumor. After her breast biopsy revealed cancer, a CT (computerized tomography) scan of the chest was performed to search for possible lung metastasis. No metastasis in the lungs as found, but a mass was seen on the inside of her heart – a rare tumor, called an atrial myxoma, was discovered that was completely unrelated to her breast cancer. Atrial myxomas are benign growths, but require open heart surgery for their removal – otherwise, pieces of the tumor can break off (embolize), travel through the bloodstream and lodge in major blood vessels causing tissue death (infarction) anywhere in the body. The most serious complications of atrial myxomas are strokes and sudden death. Sr. Rose had breast cancer, but needed heart surgery first! How was this woman, who was then 76 years old, to react? She was obviously a woman of the strongest faith and spirituality – she had devoted her life to serving God and others. She lived a life of giving – giving hope, faith, prayer, encouragement, compassion, and love to others. She never thought of herself as a person in need of anything – but now she needed something very important. She needed to have heart surgery and, soon after recovery from that, needed surgery to treat her breast cancer. Was her faith weakened by these events or strengthened to overcome these new challenges? Did she wonder why God chose her to have breast cancer and a heart tumor? Did she ever question the existence of God?

Anxiety, fear, and depression are tremendous sources of distress for cancer patients. It is important to realize the impact of fear of uncertainty in cancer patients as well as fear of dependence, abandonment, pain and, of course, death. Fear robs us of our quality of life, increases stress and makes coping with cancer more difficult and complex.

Patients with a deep spiritual belief in the afterlife find it significantly easier to overcome the fear of death. Without our spiritual beliefs, the fear of death is nearly impossible to overcome – spiritual awareness and faith provide an anchor to which we can firmly hold. Until recently, the concept of spirituality was considered to be faith-based and religious in nature. We now recognize that one's spirituality is unique and can be expressed in many different ways. Spirituality fosters hope and trust and can help cancer patients find meaning and solace through a strong spiritual foundation.

Fear and anxiety are a normal response to cancer. If untreated, excessive anxiety and fear of the unknown can increase feelings of pain and depression and diminish one's quality of life. Cancer patients often report that their fear and anxiety intensify from time to time, and are especially severe with follow up visits, x-ray and laboratory testing. Fear increases whenever a new symptom occurs or a test result is found to be abnormal. Steve, who was diagnosed with lung cancer, experienced intense, sudden and intrusive feelings of fear so severe that he was unable to process information and had difficulty making decisions about his treatment. Steve felt immobilized by his fear. He had experienced episodes of intense anxiety in college and was always concerned about his health – this became a reality with the diagnosis of cancer and plunged him into depression and a spiritual crisis. Finally, Steve decided to begin psychotherapy and approached his fear by examining his spirituality and religious beliefs. He realized that he was challenged to make the transition from superficial spirituality to solid faith. It took a giant leap of faith to overcome each hurdle but Steve persisted in surrendering his uncontrollable fears to God. The spiritual awareness and insight that Steve developed helped him find comfort in times of great struggle. His habitual ways of reacting to fear subsided and Steve started to feel at peace with himself – he realized that for years he had given credence to his fearful thoughts and, therefore, had lost his spiritual focus. Through daily prayer-meditation, journaling and therapy, Steve achieved a feeling of peace and serenity, not one of anxiety and depression. He experienced God's peace in his heart and realized that he had the strength to control his fear through increasing his hope and love for God. In the light of transformation, he was able to unburden himself and heal. In prayer, Steve was able to discover his true inner strength and to trust more fully in God. He experienced God as an ongoing, caring, and supportive presence throughout the most difficult moments in his life – a truly transforming and healing experience.

Therapeutically it is important to remove all obstacles to healing, and one of these obstacles is fear. Just as we must forgive in order to be forgiven, so we must release the fear of uncertainty in order to live in peace. Fears are learned in several ways but mostly through distortion of our thinking and beliefs. These distortions increase anxiety and depression. It is well known that fear can be aroused within minutes and therapists are taught to induce fear as a means of teaching patients how to manage their attacks. Although I never liked this form of desensitizing patients and I don't practice that way, I use this example to demonstrate how easy it is to induce a state of anxiety and fear.

Fear of the unknown in patients with cancer is very different. Cancer confronts us with a challenge like no other illness – it affects every aspect of our being. Our spiritual journey must take the course of peace, trust, faith, and hope. Spiritual teachings encourage us to overcome fear and uncertainty and to develop trust and the ability to surrender our situation into the hands of God. Faith and hope create peace in our minds and hearts. Behind our major fears is the uncertainty about what happens after we die. Healing our fear of death and dying can only be achieved through spirituality and our belief that life goes beyond the boundaries of our physical death.

Sister Rose, who was devoted to her spiritual life and trusted God in everything, struggled to hold onto her faith during the difficult times of her illness. Except for brief, insignificant illnesses, she had never been in a hospital bed. Suddenly, she was totally dependent on the people around her. Somewhere deep inside her heart, Sister Rose sensed that her life was in real danger. She allowed herself to enter a place where she had never been before: the portal of death. It was the first time in Sister Rose's life that she consciously walked into this seemingly fearful place. She realized that if she did not survive her surgery, she would enter into a new state of being. The closer she approached that fearful place, the more she realized that even there, more than ever, she was surrounded by unconditional love. She experienced an intensely personal presence, a presence so powerful and loving that she was able to push all fears aside. A presence that was filled with peace and gently said: "Don't be afraid, I will always be with you, I love you." Sister Rose felt the presence of God's spirit, simply asking her to trust Him and to surrender herself into the palm of His hand. Her whole life had been a journey with Jesus – she studied the bible for countless hours, listened to sermons and lectures, and read spiritual books. But even with all this knowledge and understanding, she never experienced the presence of Jesus as strong as that moment. He was there, the Lord of her life saying, "Come Rose trust in Me, I will not let you down". That was the moment that death lost all power and Sister Rose realized that she was held safe during the long and difficult hours of her upcoming surgery. All fear and negative feelings were swept away and she was shown that love is deeper and stronger than any fear, worry or concern about life. This experience moved Sister Rose to a new and deeper level of faith. Since her early childhood, she desired to be with Jesus. Now at the most agonizing time in her life, she felt His presence and His healing love. The God who had created her and Who knew everything about her was as close to her as He could be. She realized that, surrounded by such love and unconditional acceptance, she needed deep healing of her spirit. She journeyed back with Jesus and visited her moments of great pain and rejection until she was able to let go of all her negative emotions and pain. Sister Rose arrived at the moment of forgiveness. She became fully aware of the anguish of Jesus who lived through all she was experiencing.

After the long ordeal of her complicated surgery, Sister Rose was deeply grateful that she was alive, back among her friends and sisters in the convent. It was only in the face of her possible death that Sister Rose could clearly see what life was all about. As she sits in her armchair today, glowing with peace and love, she reflects with gratitude how much she gained from that experience. Her return to life and her struggles allows her to proclaim the love of God in a new and special way. Her greatest spiritual task was to fully and unconditionally trust God in everything and to surrender to Him. That insight was achieved in darkness and marked the time when she moved from fear to trust, from uncertainty to peace.

We must realize that we don't need to live in fear – whether we are healthy or suffer from illness, our future is always uncertain. Everyone needs to deal with fear at some level in order to live in peace. We must learn to trust in God fully, by surrendering every new morning into His caring and loving hands, trusting that He will see us through any situation we may encounter. Surrender each fearful thought when it enters your mind and replace it with a hopeful belief. It takes time to break our habitual patterns of fearful thinking, but it is possible – and it is tremendously healing!

Fear is created in our mind but can be overcome by our spiritual strength. Hope and faith come when we believe in God. The old Latin proverb *"Dum spiro, spero"* means "as long as I breathe, I hope" and emphasizes the importance of hope. Open your heart to receive the love of God – this is the deepest form of communication with the Spirit of God. Ask God to replace your restlessness, your fear, and your anxious mind with the peace that God is present, that He will give you guidance and strength to go through the valley of pain and suffering.

Surrender your thoughts, feelings, and emotions and ask God to replace your fear and anxiety with His serenity and tranquility. Invite God into your heart. Allow His divine Spirit and light to illuminate every cell of your being, uncovering all that is hidden, broken, painful and anxious. Open your heart, your soul, your spirit and body, your entire being, and your life to the healing presence of God. Feel renewed in His presence. Allow God to remove the darkness of doubt, confusion, and fear from your life. Invite Him to love and bless you, console and comfort you. Experience the light of God's healing Spirit and sense His love, compassion and mercy in your heart. God's divine light and presence has tremendous power to guide you in your life's journey – the power of the **"spirit to heal."**

CHAPTER 5

THAT FATEFUL DAY

**"Man cannot live without faith because the
prime requisite in life's adventure is courage,
and the sustenance of courage is faith."**

Harry Emerson Fosdick (1878-1969)

That fateful day arrives when the biopsy report comes
back showing cancer. Until that moment, cancer has only been a
possibility – sometimes probable, other times unsuspected.
Nevertheless, fear of the unknown is now gone. It is suddenly
and abruptly replaced by the reality of the diagnosis of cancer.
One's life has been instantly and dramatically changed forever.
Suddenly one is thrust into a state of emotional and psychological
trauma, comprised of fear, anxiety and uncertainty of the future.
It is a traumatic event, not unlike walking across the street and
being hit by an oncoming car. The trauma is life-changing. The
trauma of cancer affects one not only physically, but emotionally,
psychologically and spiritually. This particular trauma is not
fixed by healing only the physical aspect of the illness – that is,
removing the cancer is only part of the treatment on the journey
to complete healing. The emotional, psychological and spiritual
scars, questions, and challenges must also be treated for complete
healing to occur. Spiritual integrated therapy can empower one

to achieve complete spiritual healing and to access this power from deep within one's soul.

Cancer changes every aspect of one's life in ways that are not even imaginable on the day of diagnosis. The manner in which the diagnosis is conveyed to the patient by his physician is extremely important. The physician's tone of speech, degree of eye contact, posture and body language, and confidence in dealing with these critical issues are crucial in determining the initial emotional trauma suffered by the patient. In fact, the exact words used by the physician to inform his patient of this new and unwelcome diagnosis are often etched into the patient's mind forever. This tape can and often is played over and over and over again in the patient's mind. Thus, a physician who is compassionate, hopeful and confident in his approach can often allay many of the immediate fears and concerns facing his patient. An atmosphere of hope and a competent, successful plan of action against the cancer can be promoted. Alternatively, a physician who is uncertain, unclear, confusing or pessimistic can aggravate feelings of anxiety, fear, and concern for the future. A physician must never take hope from his patient and must provide one or more possible treatment plans that can be implemented in the near future to help his patient through this difficult time.

Being diagnosed with cancer is a turning point that can alter one's life but not destroy it. From that moment on, life will never be the same again – it will be different and, hopefully, more significant and meaningful. By living life with faith, hope, and a renewed sense of purpose, you can become a deeper and more exceptional person. The diagnosis of cancer is clearly traumatic but takes on a significance that can be life-changing – if we access our spiritual core. We have been asked many times if our spiritual integrated approach can work with anyone, including those who have no or very little faith. The answer is a resounding "Yes." One of our patients, a 47-year-old scientist who was diagnosed with lung cancer is a perfect example. He told me, "I have no faith and let me tell you, I have a real problem, I cannot pray. I can never find the right words to say, and why would God hear me anyhow, since I don't really have faith. But, I know I need His help. So, doctor what do you want me to do, I just can't pray?" I answered, you are praying, your suffering has become the deepest form of prayer. Surrender your pain, disappointment and anguish to God and you find yourself in the most powerful form of prayer. Spirituality and faith are unique, individual values and practices that can be expressed in many different and varied forms. Most of us take our health for granted, and many believe that with health, fitness and financial success, we have everything. But, if we don't have a heart that can love, and a soul that can reach out to others, we really have nothing at all. Cancer gives us the opportunity to change our life, to take care of unfinished business, to forgive, and to make peace with others, God, and ourselves.

Sudden death caused by a heart attack, accident or stroke interrupts one's life unexpectedly and ends relationships with acts unfinished and words unspoken. Fortunately with today's treatments, many people survive cancer and live a long and happy life. Choosing life, faith and hope can lead you to the path of healing; perhaps not always in the physical sense but certainly in the spiritual part of your being. The human body is programmed for healing. Even when your body suffers illness and your emotions are on the edge, you must remember that your spiritual being, your true inner self will not be destroyed. In contrast, giving up on life sends the wrong message, and you lose a little more life each day until your body finally stops fighting.

Your moment of trauma and shock from the diagnosis of cancer will pass with time. Remember, that during this time you will have the opportunity to touch many lives and inspire others whom you will meet on your journey. You will find that there is much to learn and to discover about yourself, including that you have an inner wisdom. With acceptance of the cancer diagnosis comes peace – fears can only be overcome with a peaceful mind and a hopeful heart. Open your spiritual eyes and see the world and the people around you in God's light and in a way you have never seen before. This is not fate, this is a turning point, an opportunity to fully surrender and return to God's love. We believe the real purpose of life is the enlightenment and healing of our spirit so that we can love better, give more, and help others on their journey. There is a deeper meaning that can only be learned through adversity – and how we deal with the challenges of adversity throughout our life.

There are many possible reactions by the patient at this important point in time, but, interestingly, the two most common are at opposite ends of the spectrum. First, a patient may become very quiet and passive and literally be in a state of mental shock. After hearing the word "cancer", these patients recall almost nothing else. They become numb to their physician and to the situation at that time. They may look at their physician with a blank stare. It is not helpful for the physician to try to force the patient to understand his medical condition when this occurs. This is not productive or helpful for either the patient or the physician. The patient is grappling with the reality of the diagnosis of cancer. In fact, even after a prolonged discussion with his physician, the patient's only question may be "So, do I really have cancer?" This is not an unexpected reaction to this devastating news, which may have come as a complete shock to the patient.

At the other end of the spectrum is the patient who has a series of multiple, detailed questions and who wants to know everything about cancer. Their questions can range from general issues regarding the development, biologic nature and treatment of cancer to very specific questions about how their cancer will affect their life. The physician needs to be understanding and compassionate and must be a trusted source of relevant information to his patient. The physician must listen to the fears and concerns of his patient and respond so that these fears and concerns can be adequately addressed. Eventually, these patients need to focus on their particular situation, but the day on which they learned their diagnosis is not the time to start limiting and directing their questions. These patients require much information in order to make a relevant and informed decision about their future treatment.

A third, but less common reaction is one of immediate acceptance of the diagnosis. These people are typically action-oriented and simply want to know the next step in order to proceed with their treatment. This response is not common because of the tremendous impact that the diagnosis of cancer and its treatments have on all phases of one's life. Nevertheless, these patients realize that this newly diagnosed disease requires treatment and, the sooner treatment is started, the sooner it will be completed. There can be an element of denial with this approach. The physical aspects of cancer treatment can be expedited with this business-like approach – however, healing of the emotional, psychologic, and spiritual scars has not yet begun. These non-physical wounds must be addressed as enthusiastically as the physical aspects of therapy so that complete spiritual healing can occur.

I will never forget a young woman, who was diagnosed with advanced non-Hodgkins lymphoma at age 32, shortly after her marriage. She was devastated and extremely sad. She had planned a new and wonderful life and was now afraid that her husband might never really get to know her, that she could not be the wife that she wanted to be for him. "What do you want him to know about you?" I asked. "Let him discover what a wonderful and courageous person you are, show him what an exceptional woman he married. And because of your cancer, you can learn to love him deeper and appreciate him for the person he is. You are a blessing to him as he is a gift to you. Never take your relationship for granted and be grateful for every day you have together. Create wonderful memories together that will never diminish and will last forever. Celebrate each moment of your togetherness. Allow him to find his strength through you and your courage, and he will grow from this. Live each moment and take every opportunity to express your love to each other. Let there be peace and let it start with you and remember that, no matter what happens, your love will never come to an end."

Many questions arise about cancer at this point in one's life. Questions such as: Why did I develop cancer? Did I do something to cause my cancer? What kinds of treatments are needed for my cancer? What are the side effects of surgery, radiation therapy and chemotherapy and am I likely to experience these complications? What is my cure rate? Will this tumor come back? Has this tumor spread to other parts of my body? Questions of paramount importance abound during this time and it becomes clear that cancer is a chronic disease that can affect one's life forever.

Many emotions can surface at this critical time in one's life, including anger, denial, depression, hopelessness, anxiety, and fear. The caring physician must recognize these emotions and provide compassion, hope, and a rational plan of treatment. Spirituality and faith offer a tremendous resource to reduce these adverse feelings. Spiritual Integrated Therapy can guide one out of the darkness of despair and anxiety and into the enlightened state of hope and peacefulness.

Information gathering on the part of the patient is necessary before an informed treatment decision can be made. The physician must have an accurate and updated knowledge of his patient's cancer and establish a relationship based on absolute trust, integrity, and honesty. He must provide accurate information at an appropriate level for the patient to completely understand his medical condition. The physician must not provide excessive or disorganized information, otherwise the patient will be confused. If confusion ensues, the patient's fears and concerns are magnified and he turns to other sources of information.

Friends, co-workers, and family members who have either had cancer or have had experience dealing with this disease commonly offer advice to the newly diagnosed cancer patient. Sometimes this advice is helpful and useful – at other times, it is unwelcome, intrusive, and inaccurate. It is difficult, if not impossible, for the patient to make a distinction between accurate or inaccurate, relevant or irrelevant, and useful or useless information regarding the biology or treatment of cancer. Friends, co-workers, and family members are generally well meaning and can certainly provide emotional support to the cancer patient. Unfortunately, the medical accuracy or relevance of their advice to a specific individual in a particular clinical situation may be lacking. For example, not all breast cancers are alike. Some are aggressive and some are very indolent; some are caused by an inherited gene and others are not; some respond well to hormone therapies and others do not; some require radiation treatment and others do not; some require treatment by a mastectomy and others can be treated by the lumpectomy approach. Cancer is a very complex disease process, and there are many variables which must be considered before prescribing a specific treatment plan.

There are now many books available to the public in large commercial bookstores dealing with all aspects of medicine, including cancer. In general, these books are helpful to provide a basic understanding of the biology and range of treatments used for different types of cancer. However, these generalizations do not apply to every cancer patient and such information must be read with this caveat in mind. There are also instances in which the information contained in these books is inaccurate or outdated. It is nearly impossible for non-medical people to determine the accuracy of such material. If a discrepancy arises between what a patient believes or understands about his disease and his physician's recommendation, the patient should question his physician for a better understanding of the rationale of the proposed treatment.

The Internet has rapidly become an important source of medical information for patients and physicians alike. Everything from chat rooms to published and unpublished research reports to clinical studies sponsored by the National Cancer Institute and other cooperative study groups can be found on the Internet. Similar to that which is found in bookstores, information on the Internet may or may not pertain to an individual patient and can be highly inaccurate. Of course, one must always consider the source of information, whether printed in book form or downloaded from the Internet.

Thus, there are many sources of information available to the patient today. It is necessary for the patient to become informed in order to make appropriate medical decisions with his physician. The physician should always be open to questions and be available as a trusted resource to resolve conflicts that may arise when patients obtain information from these varied sources. Office appointments cannot be abrupt or sessions of one-sided communication from physician to patient. Effective cancer consultation requires time, compassion, and listening to the patient's fears, concerns, and questions. Likewise, telephone calls cannot be returned to patients three or four days later. Ideally, telephone calls should be addressed that same day or, if this is not possible, early the following day. In this way, an active dialogue occurs between the patient and his physician, and a trusting, honest, and supportive doctor/patient relationship is maintained.

Only after the patient learns about his disease and the various options for its treatment can an appropriate treatment plan be developed. In some cases, few decisions need to be made as the treatment plan is clear from the outset. For example, a 64-year-old gentleman presented with rectal bleeding and underwent colonoscopy which revealed a 3 cm ulcerated cancer of the left colon. Further radiologic and blood tests revealed no evidence of metastasis, and the initial plan of treatment was surgery consisting of a left-sided colectomy. Findings at the time of surgery and final pathology results of the surgical specimen indicated that postoperative chemotherapy would be necessary. Systemic chemotherapy was administered and this gentleman is well and free of disease 4 ½ years after his initial diagnosis of cancer. In this case, the patient's presenting symptoms and stage of disease clearly dictated his treatment plan.

In other instances, significant decisions must be made before treatment is initiated. For example, the majority of women with early stage breast cancer have the option to choose between two surgical treatment options – mastectomy or breast conserving therapy. Radiation therapy is almost always combined with breast conserving therapy and consists of daily radiation treatments for approximately six weeks. In contrast, radiation is rarely used after mastectomy. All patients with breast cancer who are considering breast conserving therapy must realize this fact as it may influence their decision regarding these two options. Another example is treatment of prostate cancer in males. Early prostate cancer can be equally treated with either radiation therapy or surgery. The advantages, disadvantages, complications, and potential side effects of those two treatment options must be thoroughly discussed and evaluated prior to making an informed treatment decision.

There are many other factors, which can influence a patient's decision regarding his cancer treatment. Some are, disease-related, some are treatment-related, and others are very practical, life-related issues. For example, practical consider-ations include child-rearing responsibilities, professional and work-related issues, time and means of transportation from home to hospital, and other medical conditions that may interfere with treatment, to name only a few. The physician must be able to provide practical and relevant information to the patient to assist in making these important life adjustments. Decisions made at this time have both short- and long-term consequences for the patient, his family, friends, co-workers and his entire social network.

Challenges deepen our love to others and most certainly to God, even if we don't always feel His presence. While speaking to a support group on spirituality and healing, a young man with cancer asked me if I believed that Jesus will reveal His presence to all people who are dying. Before I was able to answer, a woman, sitting a few rows behind him said, "We all will see Jesus when He returns." She was looking to me to for approval of her statement. Instead, I paused a second and said, "Everyone waits for Jesus to return, I believe He never really left."

We find God in the most unexpected places and through others who cross our journey. The problem is that we are not always aware of His presence – often we shut Him out when life goes well. Illness and suffering give us the opportunity to open ourselves to His divine love which can sustain us through all challenges, including diseases such as cancer. This reminds me of a story about Leonardo da Vinci that has always touched me (Williamson M, 1992). Da Vinci was asked to paint a picture of Judas, who betrayed Jesus. He searched in Florence for the perfect Judas, someone who looked evil and devious enough to portray him. Eventually he found a young male with dark, cold and calculating eyes who would be the perfect model for his painting. Several years later, da Vinci was asked to paint Jesus; once again he searched the market places of Florence and found a beautiful looking young man with wonderful, warm and loving eyes. As da Vinci approached him, the young man asked: "Don't you remember me? I was the model for your painting of Judas." Da Vinci was stunned and amazed at what he saw. What he believed to be the epitome of evil had changed and reflected the love of Jesus. This story reveals the beauty and depth of the human spirit and God's presence in all of us. Jesus was already in the model of Judas, and if we look deep enough, we see the light of God in ourself and others. The spiritual light is already in us, we just need to discover it.

CHAPTER 6

BATTLING CANCER

**"For the victory of battle standeth not in
the multitude of an host; but strength
cometh from heaven."**

Apocrypha: I Maccabees 3: 18, 19

The action phase of cancer therapy can involve surgery, radiation therapy, chemotherapy, hormone therapy and experimental treatments. During the treatment phase, one has a sense of actively waging war on cancer. One is engaged in a battle to defeat cancer and must use all of the resources available to combat this formidable opponent. This battle requires energy, commitment and persistence to achieve the desired outcome – victory over disease. The battle becomes a vital part of the spiritual journey, holding onto hope and faith in the most difficult time of one's life. Without our spiritual resources, it is extremely difficult to maintain hope when the disease outcome remains uncertain. We have only one choice and that is to fight, not to surrender to cancer, fears, depression or hopelessness. In moments of weakness, we can be overwhelmed by the trauma of it all and that is why the battle against cancer is a constant one. This challenge can strengthen our spirit and sustain us through difficult times.

We continually see patients cope with cancer by having faith and hope in God and trust in the healing process. Those who are hopeful often have significantly fewer problems with anxiety and depression and cope with the disease much better compared to those who have no relationship with God. Resentment, bitterness and anger toward God, oneself or others can impair healing and, perhaps, weakened the immune system. Spiritual healing, however, is not dependent on physical health and is the deepest form of healing. If we allow the wisdom of our spirit to take over in times of weakness, our fears and uncertainties can be conquered. Our emotions clearly affect our body. Peacefulness comes through our spiritual being and is a gift of God's grace. We need a peaceful mind for healing our body and soul.

To overcome cancer, you must first accept the diagnosis and confront the disease on all fronts – physical, emotional, psychological, and spiritual. This may seem like an impossible task, but it is not. We will show you how to conquer the emotional, psychological, and spiritual consequences of this disease and to live the kind of life you would like to live. Cancer is a parasite that attempts to destroy your body, mind and spirit. You can regain control of your physical and spiritual being to combat this disease. The spiritual integrated approach empowers your spirit and strives to achieve a life of peacefulness, love, and serenity.

During the treatment phase of cancer, the physical component of your disease is attacked with strong medical therapies. Significant side effects and toxicities can occur during cancer treatment. In fact, the side effects and toxicities of cancer treatments are more severe and debilitating than those of any other disease. Expected risks of each treatment must be carefully weighed against potential benefits to determine the optimal treatment regimen for each patient. Fortunately, our body has tremendous reserve and can regenerate normal cells, including bone marrow and intestinal cells, which are rapidly dividing and especially susceptible to damage from cancer therapy. Besides the physical effects of cancer and its treatment, physicians must be attentive to their patient's fears and concerns regarding therapy. These fears may interfere with administration of therapy, aggravate its toxicity, and impair the spiritual well being of the cancer patient. Like our physical body, our emotional, psychological, and spiritual capacity has the potential to cope with these adverse, treatment-related effects. Spirituality can provide hope, faith, and freedom from fear, strengthen the immune system, increase energy level, enhance quality of life and improve our psychological well being. Many unanswered questions and issues remain in the mind of the newly diagnosed cancer patient. Next, it is time to proceed with treatment – it is time to transform from a passive patient to an active combatant against this disease.

Conventional medicine focuses its treatment on the physical aspects of disease. This is, the primary intent of medical therapy is to remove or kill cancer cells in our body. Response to treatment can be objectively measured: by physical examination, radiologic tests (e.g., chest x-ray, CT scans, or MRI) or blood tests (e.g., tumor markers such as PSA for prostate cancer, CA-125 for ovarian cancer and CEA for colorectal cancer). The body sustains tremendous physical trauma while being treated with the most powerful treatments known in the history of medicine. Although the focus must be on the physical aspects of cancer, we cannot forget the important realms of human emotion, psychology, and spirituality. It is precisely at these times when one's physical body is weakened by the effects of surgery, radiation therapy, and chemotherapy that spirituality can provide one's soul with a source of enormous strength and hope. The power of spirituality is unlimited!

The surgeon plays a critical role not only in the physical, but also in the emotional and spiritual well being of his patient. Remember the importance of the cancer diagnosis – it is generally the surgeon who informs his patient of this diagnosis. An understanding, compassionate, trusting, knowledgeable, and sincere approach can blunt the emotional and psychological turmoil at this time. The very best surgical oncologists are experts in helping their patients through this difficult time. Information must be provided in a way that is understandable to the patient and his family so that important decisions can be made and done so with informed consent. Patients and their families must feel comfortable in asking questions so that fear and anxiety are reduced or avoided. Although the physical aspects of medical care now come to the forefront, one's emotional, psychological, and spiritual needs must also be addressed.

Surgical technology has made tremendous advances in the past few decades. In fact, more progress has been made in our generation then in the entire history of medicine before that time. What today's surgeons can accomplish is truly remarkable. Advances in anesthesia and critical care medicine have paralleled progress in surgical technique so that complex procedures can be performed with greater success and fewer complications then ever before.

Incredible new surgical techniques have recently been designed to treat cancer with even faster patient recovery and fewer complications. For example, laparoscopic techniques can now be used to resect colon and kidney cancers without the need for long abdominal or flank incisions. Similar procedures in the chest are now used to resect certain lung cancers, avoiding the large, traditional chest incision. Liver resection of primary and metastatic tumors is a complex procedure associated with significant blood loss and post-operative complications. Inserting a probe into the tumors and destroying the cells with heat, by freezing, or with radio-frequency waves can now be performed to treat liver tumors. Even neurosurgery can be performed with pinpoint accuracy using the knifeless, gamma radiation approach. There is more hope than ever before in the history of mankind for today's cancer patients.

Most women with early stage breast cancer have the ability to choose between two surgical treatment options, including breast conserving surgery and mastectomy. Breast conserving surgery consists of lumpectomy and removing a portion of the axillary lymph nodes by either dissection or sentinel lymph node mapping and biopsy. With breast conserving therapy, radiation therapy is typically administered over a six-week period after complete recovery from surgery. An alternative treatment option is mastectomy or complete removal of the breast; radiation therapy is generally not needed after mastectomy surgery. Because the medical outcome of breast conserving therapy and mastectomy are equivalent for most women today, the decision regarding which procedure to pursue is often left with the patient herself. It is important to allow patients to participate in decisions when equivalent options of therapy are available. Returning some of the control back to the patient, when appropriate, allows them to actively participate in their care. It is imperative for the physician to be certain that the patient is appropriately informed and knowledgeable to make a thoughtul and reasoned decision.

Many women, but not all, will select breast-conserving therapy as opposed to mastectomy if that option exists. Mastectomy can affect women at the physical, emotional and psychological levels. Loss of the breast is often viewed as a loss in femininity. This loss can place a severe burden on one's marriage if that relationship is already weak or suffering from problems. Alternatively, in a strong, supportive relationship, couples can derive strength in the face of adversity and become closer emotionally. From a spiritual perspective, the emotional and psychological turmoil which results from this traumatic event can put one's life into perspective and establish a greater meaning or purpose for one's life.

Consider Diane, a 41-year-old female who presented with abdominal pain and bloating. On evaluation, she was found to have abdominal fluid and CT scan of the abdomen and pelvis revealed a mass in the left ovary. Blood testing revealed an elevated CA-125 of 875. She was diagnosed with ovarian cancer and underwent hysterectomy with removal of both ovaries followed by chemotherapy. As expected, this young woman was devastated and depressed after surgery – she had lost her childbearing organs and her sense of womanhood. This traumatic event can be emotionally overwhelming and can easily impair one's personal, professional, and social interactions. How can a young woman like this overcome this devastation and conquer not only her disease but also the effects of its treatment?

Let's also consider the inspiring story of Sister Rose. At

the age of 76, she was diagnosed with breast cancer. During her evaluation for metastatic disease, she was found to have a heart tumor, called a myxoma. This tumor was inside the atrium, one of the four chambers of her heart, and required open heart surgery for its removal. If the tumor was not removed, Sister Rose could have developed an incapacitating stroke, a heart attack, or even death. In reality, all of these catastrophic events could have also occurred during the surgery to remove this tumor. How was Sister Rose to cope with this devastating turn of events? She still had breast cancer, but the breast cancer could not be treated until she had surgery to remove the heart tumor. Sister Rose was raised in a family that was very religious. She grew up believing that God would always protect her from harm. She had listened for God's guidance throughout her life, so she felt the immediate need to turn to Him with the greatest struggle she ever faced. Sister Rose knew that God would be with her every step of the way. There is no doubt – the diagnosis of cancer and the discovery of a heart tumor left her devastated and in shock. Sister Rose realized that she must face this battle, and she knew that she could do this only with God's help. She was determined to fight but she knew it was not going to be easy. Every moment felt overshadowed by this battle. She remembered her life up to this point with a new sense of meaning, her love for teaching, her appreciation of nature, and her love for photography. She longed for a second chance to help others who were in the same situation, to help them appreciate life. Sister Rose wanted to give back what she had received.

From her fateful day of diagnosis, she felt she had no choice but to fight the battle against cancer and her heart tumor. She chose to fight because she chose life. Sister Rose talked to God in the childlike way she did as a young girl. She was convinced that she could learn and grow from the struggle – yet, she did not and would not know her outcome at that time. Her real battle had to do with accepting not only her diagnosis and letting go of her feeling of helplessness, but also accepting fear of the unknown. Sister Rose realized that she could be close to death. She was still afraid to die, but she experienced an inner peace that words cannot describe. She saw more and more clearly that her vocation was to acknowledge God's love and to help others deepen their faith. She now needed to use her faith in God to help her through this difficult time in her own life. Her faith and spirituality helped her tremendously in the upcoming months. Sister Rose underwent successful heart surgery to remove the atrial myxoma and four months later she underwent mastectomy to treat her breast cancer. She is alive and well and an inspiration to all of us who know her. Current and future generations of people will be empowered by her hope and faith and by her amazing and courageous story.

Cancer knows no boundaries for age, sex, race, religion, or socioeconomic status. Ken, a 65-year-old man, was diagnosed with prostate cancer. He was told that his prostate cancer was caught early and very likely to be cured. The two possible treatment options included radical surgery (to remove the prostate gland and pelvic lymph nodes) or radiation therapy. Despite obtaining much information about these two treatment options, he was uncertain whether to undergo surgical resection or radiation therapy. He wavered back and forth with his decision. His intuition told him to undergo surgery, to cut the tumor out – he felt safer that way. However, the possible side effects from surgery were just too great, including impotence and voiding dysfunction. Would his relationship with his wife suffer if he became impotent from surgery? He had been happily married for

37 years but now had serious questions that had never occurred to him before. As you can see, the consequences of his decision extended far beyond the physical treatment of his prostate cancer – it affected his manhood and could potentially impact his relationship with his wife.

Like surgery, radiation therapy provides treatment to a localized region of the body. Radiation therapy has become incredibly sophisticated in the recent era of high technology. Computers manipulate complex equations of radiation biology, and physicists work closely with clinicians to plan radiotherapy for cancer patients on a daily basis. Even before the first dose of radiation is given, treatment planning (or simulation) takes several days of extensive analysis and preparation. As a result, improved accuracy of radiation therapy has produced increased treatment success and fewer side effects than ever before.

A typical course of conventional radiation therapy is five days per week for approximately six weeks. Thus, radiation therapy is administered over a protracted period of time – in this way, radiation therapy is unlike surgery. This difference is significant from a practical point of view, as well as from an emotional and psychological perspective. The patient must be able to travel to and from the radiation facility on a daily basis for six weeks – this has important personal, professional, and social implications. Consider the 39-year-old single mother with breast cancer who lives 45 minutes from the hospital; she needs a six week course of radiation therapy to complete her treatment of breast cancer. Think about the 58-year-old chief financial officer of a major bank in town who requires lung surgery followed by radiation therapy to the chest wall. What about the 48-year-old housewife who underwent colon resection and now needs radiation to the left side of her abdomen and pelvis? Besides the actual 30 or more trips to the hospital to receive radiation therapy, emotional, psychological, and spiritual demands are placed on one's life – as well as the lives of one's family, friends, and co-workers. How is one to deal with the ongoing trauma created and sustained by this protracted treatment of cancer?

We have many wonderful and courageous patients who touch our lives every day. Their determination and faith show that prayer is powerful and encourage other patients who are struggling with their own challenges. Through their struggles with cancer, they find a deeper and fuller appreciation of life and themselves. They learn to heal, to overcome their difficulties, to love, to hope and to have faith. By choosing this path of healing, they make a commitment to faith, to God, and to life. As long as we can love and feel loved, our life has true purpose; and as long as we can pray for others in this world, our spirit is healing. The moment we live in fear, doubt and confusion, our spiritual, physical and mental equilibrium is thrown out of balance. We must choose faith over fear, hope over doubt, and clarity over confusion – and most of all, we must live in the spirit of love. Everyone responds to love in a healing way during times of illness. Spiritual strength can sustain you in the days and months ahead when important decisions must be made regarding cancer treatment. It is important to have a peaceful mind and a prayerful attitude to heal at the emotional, psychological and spiritual levels.

Radiation therapy has potential short- and long-term side effects. Short-term effects typically include redness, irritation, and superficial burning of the skin through which the radiation is given. Scatter of radiation to nearby organs can cause damage to the heart, lungs, bones, small or large intestine, bladder, and other structures in the direct path of the radiation beam – however, this collateral damage has been dramatically reduced with the increased precision of modern radiotherapy techniques. Fatigue, dry mouth, pain with swallowing, diarrhea, and decreased circulating blood cells can occur and is usually time-limited.

Chronic or long-term side effects can include pain and tenderness at the site of treatment, swelling or lympedema at or adjacent to the site of radiation, and dysfunction of organs and tissues near the radiation site. Again, significant dysfunction of adjacent organs and tissues is uncommon with today's sophisticated technology and precise treatment planning.

New techniques are constantly being tested and applied to clinical practice. Brachytherapy is a technique which gives high intensity radiation therapy directly to the tumor site. Radiation injury to adjacent, normal tissues is minimized and side effects are reduced. Conformal radiation is another way to provide very precise radiation by external beam to a specific site in the body, again with minimal effect to surrounding tissues. In fact, the exact location of an individual's particular tumor can be programmed and targeted for therapy with very little spread outside the tumor mass itself. For example, the precise configuration of a specific prostate cancer can be treated without radiating non-cancerous portions of the prostate gland. Other possibilities include implanting radioactive seeds directly into the tumor to provide maximal therapy with the least possible damage to normal tissues.

Chemotherapy is perhaps the most dreaded of all cancer treatments. Why is this so? It is because chemotherapy, unlike surgery and radiation therapy, is a systemic treatment – that is, it affects the entire body. Chemotherapy is designed to spread throughout the body to kill cancer cells wherever they are located – its side effects are widespread as well. Chemotherapy works on the principle of killing replicating or dividing cells – that is, cells that are actively making (or synthesizing) DNA, RNA, or protein. DNA and RNA are nucleic acids which code cellular information, and proteins are functional or structural molecules required for living cells to grow and replicate. The major flaw with conventional chemotherapy, however, is that it is non-specific. Chemotherapy cannot distinguish between cancer cells and normal cells. Toxicity results from the effects of chemotherapy on normal cells and, in fact, to achieve the greatest tumor response, chemotherapy is often pushed to the limits of toxicity.

Toxicity of chemotherapy is widespread and can affect any organ or system within the body, depending upon the type of chemotherapy used. Typically the most rapidly dividing cells in the body are the most susceptible to chemotherapy. Bone marrow cells and intestinal cells normally have rapid replicating rates and damage to these cells can cause significant toxicity. Bone marrow suppression causes infection, bleeding, easy bruisability, and fatigue. Damage to gastrointestinal cells causes nausea, vomiting, diarrhea, abdominal discomfort, pain with swallowing and oral ulcers. Many other side effects are possible with chemotherapy including hair loss (alopecia), allergic reactions, neuromuscular symptoms, cystitis, electrolyte imbalances, liver toxicity, kidney failure, and cardiac toxicity.

Fortunately for cancer patients today, many types of chemotherapy-related toxicity can be prevented or drastically reduced. For instance, clinical studies of many different cancers have shown that short courses of chemotherapy are just as effective as long, protracted treatment regimens. Since duration of exposure to these agents is limited, less toxicity occurs. Second, improved understanding of the metabolism of chemotherapy agents has led to the design of more effective and less toxic treatment schedules. Often, complete courses of treatment can be given as outpatient therapy – this sharply contrasts with treatment only a few years ago when hospitalization was standard for chemotherapy administration. Third, medications have been developed to reduce or eliminate many chemotherapy-related toxicities. Some medications provide relief of general symptoms such as nausea, vomiting, or diarrhea. Other agents are very specific in their action – for example, colony-stimulating factors directly increase production of red blood cells, white blood cells, and platelets to prevent anemia, infection, and bleeding from damage to the bone marrow. These agents not only prevent toxicity but can be life-saving at times. Finally, tremendous progress in molecular biology and cellular genetics has led to an explosion in the development of new cancer therapies. These innovative therapies are much more specific than conventional chemotherapy and can target a precise molecule or receptor located on the cancer cell. Great potential exists for molecular therapy of cancer to increase tumor response and decrease patient toxicity in the future.

Clinical trials are another important component of cancer treatment regimens today and in the future. Cancer centers that participate in clinical trials provide therapy at the leading edge of cancer research. It is essential to understand how these studies work if one is considering treatment on clinical trial. There are three phases of clinical trials, depending on the stage of development of the experimental treatment being tested.

Phase I clinical trials evaluate the toxicity of new treatments. The primary purpose of Phase I trials is to determine the dose of the experimental therapy to be used in future studies. Of all the phases of clinical trials, tumor response to agents under

Phase I study is the lowest. Phase II trials are designed to test the activity of new treatments in causing tumor response. This phase of study determines whether or not new therapies are effective and what tumor types are most responsive. Phase III studies are conducted after encouraging results are obtained in Phase I and II trials. Phase III trials compare tumor response of the experimental treatment to the best available treatment for a specific type of cancer. Phase III trials typically randomize (or assign) patients between the different treatments being studied and hold the best chance for tumor response of all the phases of clinical research.

New cancer therapies are being developed worldwide at a faster pace than ever before. Recent advances in biotechnology provide hope for even greater success to develop more effective and less toxic treatments in the next few years. By uniting the worlds of science and spirituality, we believe that improved quality of life, reduced anxiety and fear, and enhanced spiritual growth can be achieved. The future is more promising than ever before in the history of mankind to conquer the physical aspects of this devastating disease. Faith, hope, and spirituality can augment conventional medicine in treating the cancer patient and have the potential to provide us with the **spirit to heal**.

CHAPTER 7

PERSONAL GROWTH AND TRANSFORMATION

"Life's a voyage that's homeward bound."

Herman Melville (1819 – 1891)

Cancer is an unwelcome intruder into our life. It is harmful and destructive to our body – but, it offers us an incredible opportunity to strengthen our spirit and awaken our soul. Our spiritual journey of transformation typically begins with an event of great sadness and suffering – we are called to this spiritual path for it is not a planned or conscious decision. It is a divine call from God to get closer to Him and, in doing so, we also get closer to others around us.

The spiritual journey is a transforming process that leads to the healing of our thoughts, expectations, motives, and feelings toward God, others, and ourselves. When we begin our spiritual journey, we learn to trust God beyond our psychological experiences. Perception by the human spirit is far more sensitive than that of the human mind. Once we are on our spiritual journey, we begin to perceive that our emotions, reactions and motives toward other people and ourselves come from a place of deep hurt. The function of the human spirit is to forgive these hurts and to learn important lessons from them. If we can learn through our challenging life experiences, such as tragedies, illness, and losses, then our life is a success. The spiritual journey can be a lonely road in the beginning – but, God does not take anything away without giving us something better in return. In the beginning, some doors will open and others will close – and, sometimes, one door will open and we are then faced with a hundred closed doors. These periods of struggle and decision move us to new levels of understanding and can move us to a closer relationship to God, ourselves, and others. We begin to see the world from a different perspective. We see that our thoughts and speculations remove us from the immediacy of our experience. Our mental capacities are an extraordinary gift, but can also be constricting when used to retreat from contact with ourselves and others. To heal spiritually, our mind must be open to learn, to grow, and to transform during our spiritual journey.

The goal of our spiritual life is the recovery of our spiritual essence. Facing sickness, trials, and losses can often leave us emotionally, mentally, and physically debilitated. During our emotional or mental lows, we build emotional defense mechanisms. These defenses act like barriers that hinder us from loving, having compassion and being truly focused on other people around us. These defenses are rarely consciously built, but can arise almost instantly. We can be so wounded that our reaction is to withdraw to protect ourselves from ever feeling that pain again. These defensive barriers have power over our mind, our physical actions, and our emotional responses. It is not unusual for people who have experienced great emotional hurts to numb themselves, to avoid feeling more pain. But, sadly it is not only the pain they don't feel – instead, all the other feelings we need to sustain our relationships also become numb. They do not experience true happiness or love – they are emotionally detached. It is not unusual that a 55-year-old man is unable to feel, to cry or to express his deepest needs and emotions. He was taught at an early age not to express deep feelings and he learned to repress his feelings. Fifty years later, when he tries to express these emotions, it is an almost impossible task.

The process of personal growth is not easy – we must first face our pain and release it. When we ask God to help us heal our lives, God may allow people to enter our lives who have something to teach us – they can inspire us, give us encouragement, provide a new life experience and offer a depth of love that is very new to us. At times we are frightened by goodness and too many blessings. Instead of appreciating them, we start to explain them away with doubtful comments such as "it's only accidental", "what a coincidence", or "this can't be real." But, the greatest blessing is that we learn to access places in our heart which have been untapped for a lifetime – we have that extraordinary capacity. We progress in a new direction and must stop to re-think the value systems, the goals and the ultimate purpose of our life. God will introduce us to people to help us evolve, to heal and to transform. On this spiritual journey, we hand our lives over to the Spirit of God and surrender to His plan and guidance. People who come into our lives are there for a purpose – it is no coincidence. God knows exactly what we need and meeting with people who will teach us and help us to change is part of our journey. Those whom we have met on our journey will be there, because together we have the potential for a holy relationship. Not everyone who is placed into our lives will be perceived as a blessing. Sometimes they present a challenge but these people can become a blessing when we have met that challenge and learned a valuable lesson. Often the ones who have hurt us the most become our greatest teachers. They teach us a very important lesson – that is, the lesson of true forgiveness, of letting go, of not closing our hearts in bitterness or deep resentment. Forgiveness is essential for personal growth and true spiritual transformation.

Spiritual growth is never about focusing on someone else and their lives, but requires that we reflect on our own life. We sometimes believe that we cannot forgive certain actions in our minds and even in our hearts. But, in the immense depth of our human spirit where we are truly connected to God, we can act in that Godly love and reach out to forgive and to let go. When we learn to forgive, we move from resentment to compassion and from hate to love – we create the power of the **spirit to heal**. It is not easy to forgive people who have hurt us to the core of our being, but it is essential for attaining true spiritual healing. Not only do these individuals test the limits of our capacity for forgiveness, but they can impede us from forgiving and make it difficult for us to achieve spiritual transformation. The choice to forgive is a choice for God's love. No matter how difficult it may seem, when we forgive that way we will automatically place the other person in God's light. God asks us to forgive. In fact, God wants us to forgive first so that we too can be forgiven.

We are often unwilling to forgive because it may mean becoming vulnerable again to those who hurt us. Does forgiveness mean that we must act as though nothing happened, that we should forgive and forget? No, it does not. We must learn from these encounters to progress on our spiritual journey. We need to forgive and we need to be forgiven in order to heal completely. Without forgiveness, spiritual healing is impossible.

Resentment and bitterness can have deep roots in our human heart. Unforgiveness of our spirit has certain symptoms that can affect us physically, mentally, and spiritually. There is no better way to alleviate deep resentment and guilt than the power of forgiveness. A strong relationship exists between our spiritual and physical health. All intense emotions like self-hate, resentment, and anger toward others need to be released. We must to release these emotions and the people connected to these emotions to the Spirit of God. Being able to do so will surrender the entire situation, everyone involved, every feeling, and every emotion to God's divine spirit. Holding onto these negative life events has a price – we can re-experience past trauma and hurt for years to come. We come to a standstill and feel that our life is not moving forward, we are stuck in a rut and become anxious and depressed. Forgiveness is extraordinarily valuable and will shift our thinking from hate to love and from revenge to compassion. While you are reading these pages, perhaps someone will come into your mind, like a snapshot or a brief image of someone you knew or perhaps still know. This experience is often God's reminder that we need to lift that person up to be forgiven or we may need to ask that person for forgiveness. We have all experienced a person from the past suddenly entering our minds for no known reason. Perhaps it is someone we met years ago, perhaps someone we have not seen for 20 or 30 years. When that person enters your mind, release that person and all the feelings you have connected with that experience to the Spirit of God. That it is part of the divine plan – that person may need your prayers, your love, or your forgiveness.

Some people are sent to us, "God sent," to bring light, love, joy, insight, and wisdom into our lives. These people will help us stay on our journey, and we must pray for them as they help us to stay on our path of growth and transformation. We must never forget to keep them in our hearts and prayers and we must never abandon anyone in pain. These are holy encounters which are meant to teach us, to help us grow, and to help us open our hearts to love more deeply. We can only feel that something divine is happening in our spirit. Logically, these experiences make no sense and could easily be ascribed to coincidence. But no divine encounter, no person that God ever chooses to enter our lives, is a coincidence.

We experience an emotional freedom and a release of guilt and fear when we forgive. Forgiveness is extremely important for healing our emotions and so many times, its effect is underestimated or considered unimportant. In fact, in modern psychiatry, we cannot find the word forgiveness or unforgiveness in psychiatric textbooks. The inability to forgive creates enormous guilt, emotional turmoil, bitterness and unnecessary anger. It can affect one so severely that, after years of caring and love, one appears bitter, angry, and resentful. In direct contrast, nothing makes us glow and radiate as much as love. When we love, we are directly connected to the very source of God. How many people have we met in our lifetimes that just shine? They may not be very successful or have accomplished great things, but they are radiant and their eyes are warm and full of love. Being in the presence of such love and light touches one's heart and soul. I remember in one of my lectures, I guided the audience through a forgiveness meditation and one young woman, who came with her friend, prayed at that moment that she would be able to have a baby. She had unsuccessfully been on a fertility program for 11 years. She and her husband decided two months before not to continue with the fertility program and they decided to adopt a child. In her forgiveness meditation, she released her father and several other people she had not forgiven for many years and told me later that she had felt a tremendous peace in her heart. Twelve days later she called me with excitement to inform me that her pregnancy test came back positive, and she was certain that the healing seminar had much to do with that outcome. "I know exactly the moment of conception, there was no other moment than the evening after the seminar, and I know something so profound happened in me that I was given this gift." On a physical level what actually happened here may never be fully explained, but on a spiritual level, she is convinced that God gave her a little miracle, and that little miracle was born two months ago.

Forgiveness is so powerful that it can immediately release blocked emotions. Often our mind perceives that a particular emotion has gone away, but intense emotions once stored in the body will not resolve or disappear by repressing or denying them. Forgiveness is a powerful way of releasing negative emotions and the entire experience associated with them. When we are released from that pain, we experience a peace and freedom the world cannot provide in any other way.

Sometimes in life when we are faced with a real crisis, such as cancer, we need to forgive God. Why? Because deep in our hearts, often our first reaction to the diagnosis of cancer is that we hold Him responsible. Some patients even believe that they were given this disease as punishment for something they did wrong. We do not believe that God created cancer or purposefully gives cancer to the people He loves. God never promised that He will not present us with sickness or trials or hardships or challenges. In fact, He told us that we need to go through trials and tribulations to grow and to learn. But, He will sustain us and provide us with the strength and endurance to overcome these challenges. With cancer, some cases can be cured by enduring difficult treatments. In others, cancer cannot be cured from our physical body but our spirit will grow, transform, and heal. We must realize that in death, we are born into a new existence, and we unite with God. The greatest healing often does not happen in our physical body, but in our spirit. It is our spirit, not our body, that will ultimately communicate with God. Cancer should never be seen as a punishment, but can be viewed as a challenge for spiritual growth, transformation and surrender to His work.

Working with cancer patients is most rewarding and a continuing source of hope and faith. By watching God sustain our patients through physical and emotional suffering, we strongly believe that God is very real and very present in their lives. I remember years ago receiving a phone call at 2:30 a.m. on a cold winter's night. It was my patient's husband calling me from the hospital to tell me that his wife, a brilliant musician who was 45 years old, was just told that she was nearing the end of her life from cancer. He asked me if I would come to the hospital to see her and to be with her when she passed on. I remember driving for about 45 minutes on freshly fallen snow to the hospital, and I was praying that Lynn would wait for me. It was impossible to drive any faster and the snow increased, but I knew deep in my heart that God would not take that opportunity away from me and certainly not from Lynn. As I entered the room, I saw her husband and daughter sitting at her bedside. I was suddenly overcome with a deep sense of a divine presence in Lynn's room, something I had never felt before. The room was filled with such peace and love that I was moved to tears. As I approached Lynn's bed I suddenly sensed the presence of two large, beautiful angels standing on either side of her bed. The angels were placing their arms gently underneath Lynn's very frail body, just as though they were ready to lift her up. I was in such awe of this image that I was not sure how to tell Lynn or her family what I was experiencing. I wondered at the time if I was seeing a vision or if I was creating a picture in my own mind. I did not want to question what I was experiencing, it was just too beautiful. As I walked toward Lynn I felt incredibly blessed to be part of such a divine encounter. She smiled at me and I could see the peace in her face. I gently took her hand and I said, "Lynn, I am right here with you." She whispered my name and asked me to come a little closer because it was difficult for her to speak. Lynn said, "I just had the most wonderful experience, I think I am in a dream." I asked her if she wanted to tell me what she was experiencing, and she told me that she saw two beautiful, tall and strong angels at the either side of her bed. They were waiting to lift her up to heaven. These angels were so beautiful and radiant that she felt peaceful and loved, and she was ready to leave. I was so deeply moved by what she was describing because it was exactly what I had sensed when I entered her room. I told her that I had seen the same vision and that I had sensed a divine presence that illuminated her room. Lynn looked over to her husband and said, "I think it is time honey for me to go, I want to go, they are all waiting for me." She was surrounded by her family when she peacefully parted with this world several hours later. I will never forget this experience.

I do believe with my whole heart that these angels lifted her gently to heaven. What Lynn taught me that night is never to doubt these divine moments, never to brush them off as a coincidence or some illusion that we just can't explain. This experience taught me to take these divine visions or images seriously. I have related Lynn's experience to so many of our cancer patients, and I hope she smiles each time from the wonderful place that she is knowing that her experience helps so many who fear dying alone. In fact, I believe that we are never alone in moments of pain or suffering. I believe that angels, departed loved ones, our family, our friends, and others we've met on our life's journey will come to greet us and help us in our time of need. We must never forget to call on them in moments of need, in moments of anguish, and in moments of pain.

As doctors we must recognize the awareness and sensibility of the human spirit. We must never dismiss a vision or a spiritual experience as something that has been imagined or produced as a side effect of a medication or treatment. Elizabeth Kuebler-Ross described a remarkable story in one of her books, Life after Death, from a research study of approximately 50 patients who were born blind (Kuebler-Ross E, 1991). None of these patients were ever able to see a ray of sunshine, a flower, or the colors of a rainbow. As they grew older, one particular woman had a major stroke and a near death experience. She died for a brief period of time and was then resuscitated back to life. This woman was amazed by all the things she was able to see when she was thought to be clinically dead. She saw the room, she saw a blue folder on her bedside table, she could describe what the people looked like in the room, and, yet, when she came back to her life, she was still blind. She only saw these things when she was thought to be dead. This story touched me so deeply because it confirms to me that when God says we are perfected in death, we are truly restored to perfection by God after death. After leaving our physical body and this world, we enter into the beauty and perfection of our human spirit.

Our birth, our death and our life in between are divine creations – part of our spiritual journey. Consciously, we cannot remember our birth or the day we entered into this world. But, the experience of our death may be the most extraordinary experience we will ever have. Regardless of how we die, I do believe that people are comforted so that they can pass gently into the arms of God – even in moments of a painful death, God is comforting. I have known many people who were severely injured and yet survived their injuries – looking back at the moment of their accident, they cannot recall pain. They cannot recall what happened, and this illustrates how God has magnificently designed the body, the mind and the spirit. He allows us to have only as much pain as we can tolerate – not more.

Modern psychology commonly examines only two levels of human existence, the conscious and the subconscious (or unconscious) mind. Although recognizing these two levels of existence, Spiritual Integrated Therapy is based upon enlightenment at one's innermost core, at the soul level. Faith, hope, love, and forgiveness are integral components of this spiritually based approach. True healing requires transformation of the human spirit, taking a challenging and, at times, difficult path.

The physical world is not our final home. This world is just a place to grow and to learn, to love and to forgive, so that we can enter our real home – our spiritual home. The human soul, as we understand it, is that part of our being in which our spirit resides. If our soul has been damaged by a lack of love, affection, or nurturing, our spirit may find it difficult to develop and grow close to God. That is why forgiveness is so essential in the healing process. We have to recall and to forgive resentment, judgment, hate, and anger that we developed earlier in life to be released from these emotions that can repress our spirituality.

The laws and axioms which govern our physical world are fixed and rigid, unlike the nature of human behavior. For instance, physicists know that for every action, there is an equal and opposite reaction. The law of gravity is constant. Chemists know that formulas of chemical reactions must balance; this is a basic chemical principle. Man must breathe to maintain his physical existence – he must also eat and sleep. That is absolute fact for our physical existence on this earth.

Our behavior is not regulated by such unyielding laws. Each one of us is free to make his own choices. Although we are not required to act a certain way, we are responsible for our choices and there are consequences for our actions. We can't blame others or God for what we have chosen and how we react to life situations. God does not free us from resentment when we elect to retain it. The more clearly we have insight into our self, the more likely we are to release our old limiting patterns of behavior from the past. As we let go of these behaviors, our awareness expands and our sense of self shifts. Our own personal development progresses, and we uncover deeper truth about our personality and our spiritual nature. It is important to understand our spiritual nature, as we each possess a unique and beautiful spirituality. Our spirituality can hinder us from accessing the innermost depth of our being and connecting with God or, on the contrary, it may enable us to do so. All of us are looking for answers to some of life's most difficult problems. We may express ourselves in different ways, but at some common human level, we are all seeking a way to lead a richer, more fulfilling, loving, and graceful life – and trying to help others do the same. Understanding ourselves on a profound spiritual level is important to developing a deeper and more genuine spirituality.

Learning to observe ourselves and releasing old habits is difficult, but we must never forget that we are on a spiritual path. No spiritual journey can be followed without self-transcendence or transformation. We must change in order to progress. Many of us are absorbed only in ourselves, like body builders who focus on the development of only one aspect of their physique instead of seeking overall balance. How many times have we abandoned ourselves and rejected our own heart's desires to be the kind of person we believe will be more acceptable and worthwhile? Yet, unknowingly we bring out what we most fear – that is, the fear of being worthless, helpless and valueless. Genuine intimacy with someone is especially threatening when we don't believe that we are lovable, valuable, and worthy. Intimacy is the willingness to share oneself totally with another person without holding back affection, appreciation, and most of all love. That is why we need to find our true spiritual essence and to break habits and behaviors that limit our spiritual growth. Only then are we able to commit ourselves to another and to progress on our spiritual journey.

We learn in our spiritual journey to use our abilities to affirm the value of others, which allows them to experience their own true value. That is the most beautiful gift we can give to anyone, and a gift that will be deeply appreciated by them. When we open our hearts spiritually to the people close to us, we discover real sources of self-esteem. We discover that we have something to give, that we can encourage others and be affirmative, loving, and supportive. Being in touch with the goodness in our own heart fills us with so much joy and serenity that we should never return to our old ways. Our spiritual being is not concerned about impressing others with prestige, success, or symbols of earthly status. Deep spiritual healing will touch every part of our being. It involves our thoughts, our feelings, our actions, our desires, and the lives of others in a profound way. Perhaps you have experienced a connection with someone that was immediate and profound – you cannot explain what actually happened and why you felt so deeply connected. But you experienced awareness of your spirit and the spirit of another, someone with whom you feel comfortable – and it goes beyond comfort, it becomes a relationship, a friendship, a partnership or even a marriage that is of oneness. A relationship formed with God's purpose to complete one another, that is the ultimate love, and a relationship that can never be broken. This type of relationship is only possible when we connect spiritually, and there is nothing more exiting and fulfilling to the human soul. Physical or intellectual attraction alone can never replace spiritual unity. That unity, that holy encounter, will exist beyond this life. It will continue eternally and strengthen as those individuals and spirits grow together. Every healthy relationship needs to grow – if it doesn't grow and evolve over time, then even a good relationship will deteriorate.

The relationships and encounters that are formed on the spiritual level will sustain us through difficult periods of our life, such as times of great pain, suffering, or fear. Our intelligence, our physical strength and our superficial friendships or relationships cannot do so. In fact, during our most difficult times, we may find that these superficial relationships deteriorate and we find strength, support, and peace with others who connect with us on a deep spiritual level. Is this a coincidence or chance happening? No, it is divine intervention guiding us along our spiritual journey of self-transcendence. We can then unconditionally accept ourselves and unconditionally accept others. Then, it is possible for us to give something deeper, more personal and more gratifying to others than we have ever done before – we have been transformed. We are no longer conflicted by former motives such as the desire to be loved, our self-esteem, our need to please others to feel good about ourselves. We will awaken our soul and become free of these self-centered motives that directed our thoughts, feelings and actions for so long.

While there is life, there is hope. Hope reflects the deepest and most essential instinct of our human nature, regardless of nationality, religion, or culture. Hope is a primordial dimension of the soul which must be nurtured. It is essential that we expect something from our future – if not, we will have difficulty praying and connecting with God. Our spiritual journey stops as our own life stands still – do not waste these precious moments. Prayer is healing and can help guide us on our spiritual journey. Prayer is hope for our spirit – whether we pray in church or elsewhere and whether we pray for a few minutes or hours. The most important aspect of prayer is that we pray from our heart and soul with a certainty and conviction that God hears us. Then, we have truly been transformed.

CHAPTER 8

RELATIONSHIPS AND SUPPORT

**"All loves should be simply stepping-stones to the
love of God. So it was with me; and blessed be
his name for his great goodness and mercy."**

Plato (ca 422 – 347 B.C.)

Cancer does not affect just one person – it is much more far-reaching and pervasive than that. Cancer affects one's family friends, co-workers and everyone with whom the cancer patient has a close or significant relationship. The emotional and psychological turmoil of the patient can be felt by each of these individuals and can profoundly alter their relationships. In some instances the relationship becomes stronger, more committed and more intense – these people can be a source of tremendous support and strength for the cancer patient and can promote the **spirit to heal**. In contrast, the diagnosis of cancer can stress one's relationships and weaken or even destroy a fragile or damaged relationship. Both the healing and destructive effects on these relationships can be permanent, life-changing events.

Even those with the strongest faith and spirituality are challenged in these difficult times. For Sister Rose it was the loving community of sisters who received her with open arms after her surgery and her struggle to hold on to life. Surrounded by such love and friendship, she was able to restore her being, heal her spirit, and find immense joy and peace. But even when everything seemed ideal, Sister Rose needed a safe place to hit bottom. Just when she was in the prime of her spiritual life and praised for her spiritual insights, she felt somehow devoid of faith. Just when people were thanking her for bringing them closer to God, she felt deep inside that God had abandoned her. The anguish Sister Rose felt took her completely by surprise – it was something she had never experienced before. Surrounded by love, God allowed her to plunge into the darkness of her own fears. Everything came crashing down – her self esteem, her faith, her energy, her sense of being loved, her hope for healing, even her trust in God, everything. It was as if all that had given her life meaning had been stripped away. Intellectually Sister Rose knew that no human friendship could fulfill the deepest longing of her heart. She knew that only God could give her what she desired. The mystery of God's presence can be touched only by the sense of His absence. Yet, she knew that God was with her in every dimension of her life, even in her fear. God revealed himself through prayer, friendship, and her love for nature. To her surprise she never lost the ability to see the beauty of the world through her camera. Sister Rose is a nature photographer. God guided her to open her camera lens widely for breathtaking scenes of snow capped mountains, animals and tall, strong trees. She realized that God had given her all these beauties and wonders of creation with love.

Sister Rose has the most beautiful photographic collection of butterflies. Why the butterfly? The butterfly symbolizes unity, love, new life, and resurrection. She began to trust again that her experience of emptiness was not a finality and that beyond is a wonderful place where she is held in love. It is precisely at this moment that we make a transforming discovery – that is, the more love we experience, the less fearful we become. We begin speaking more through our actions, using fewer words, and expressing ourselves more directly, without fearing the reactions of others. For Sister Rose, sharing her struggle and anguish became a service to others. She offers courage, hope, wisdom, faith and inspiration to all who share her journey.

True affection and genuine love is not superficial – it is healing, deeply and emotionally rooted, and profoundly spiritual. How can one communicate such intense feelings to another? One of the most therapeutic ways to express deep emotions or feelings is to put them in writing. Not just our complex emotions, such as fear or anger or grief, but overwhelming feelings of love and affection can also be expressed this way. To write a letter to someone you deeply love is very important and is a written commitment at the soul level – it is one of the most powerful ways to express how we genuinely feel. Unfortunately, our generation has largely abandoned the art of letter writing. Through computer technology, e-mail, fax, telephone and other fast communications, the art of expressing our love in a very special letter to someone has deteriorated. In poetry, love letters reign among writers' finest achievements, as if one's beloved is required to inspire the best poetry. A number of famous writers and poets – including Kafka, Rilke, and Kleist – had love affairs that existed only in correspondence (Davidson CN, 1996). A love letter fulfills a need to confide, to verify, and to articulate what is ordinarily left unspoken.

For at least some writers and poets, the love letter may well be the ultimate literary act. The craft of literature teaches one how to entice with words and how to view the world through the eyes of the writer (Barry J, 1987). Many lovers feel renewed by love and record their rebirth in love letters. Love letters transform us (Givner J, 1982). There are few things as beautiful as holding a letter from someone we deeply love. It is important that we leave a love letter to everyone for whom we care deeply – a mother to her children, a father to his son, a husband to his wife. Poet John Keats distills the sense of love's eternal timelessness into one of the most beautiful images in a letter he wrote to the woman he loved, Fannie Brawne (Scudder H, 1899). Keats wished that he and his lover could be butterflies together for just three days – since happiness in this loving union could far surpass many years without such love. Keats expressed clearly that it wasn't the length of years we have on this earth, but the intensity, importance and significance of time. It is true – butterflies live for only three days; and true love can be filled with more love and emotion in three days than a lifetime without such feeling. Think about that concept for just a moment – it's profound and it is true.

A long life does not necessarily mean a wonderful life, nor does perfect health mean happiness. Our achievements mean very little if we have no one who appreciates us beyond our worldly accomplishments. What gives our life significance and meaning is the love we share with others and the way we live and express that love. We have a wonderful opportunity in a love letter to express our thoughts and our feelings in the deepest way possible. How many times have we encountered situations when someone has passed away and the first question was "What were his last words?" A letter will touch our loved ones forever and I suggest that as you read this, you think about the people who mean the most to you at this moment and write their names on a piece of paper. Choose the first person to whom who you would like to write a letter and before you write, just pray – pray to God to give you the right inspiration to find the words to express your affection, your love, and your gratitude for that person. Then sit down in a comfortable place, preferably in front of window with a view to nature, start your thoughts and just let your hand and pen do the writing. The love and energy that pores out in that letter can never be destroyed. In fact, the reader will be deeply touched by your words.

Love encourages, gives strength, joy, hope and faith. A true relationship is not blind or naïve; it sees both the good and the not so good, and loves anyway. True oneness happens not by obliterating someone nor by inflating oneself over the other, but by surrendering every aspect of our motives and desires to God (Sandford J, Sandford P, 1985). Oneness is not control of each other but the delight of two people enjoying, discovering and experiencing God's purpose, wonder and blessings that He has placed before them. In true oneness, we achieve a symphonic harmony where two individuals are free to be themselves, spontaneous and open, yet interwoven as one melody. Oneness is not a loss of individualism as often taught in modern psychology; it is when hearts and minds connect so that the tiniest clues and nuances are understood. The goal is to live and bless each other, walking through life together with all its joys and heartbreaks, joined and yet secure as individuals. It is marked by laughter and ease of heart, nothing heavy, nothing intense. Trust in your partner and trust in God that everything will work out for the best. Only in this oneness can we truly appreciate our partner's accomplishments and talents.

Oneness is also feeling each other's pain and losses. More than our emotions grieve when someone we love is hurt. Sorrow has a strength when it is shared in love for the other. It is important for a couple to face the trauma of cancer together. Any form of rejection, physically, sexually or emotionally is one of the greatest harms a person with cancer can experience. It intensifies anxiety, uncertainty, and depression and can easily cause problems in one's relationship. A couple must work together to overcome the difficulties of cancer by coming together, not by growing apart. A marriage or relationship suffers when couples become insensitive or withdraw from each other. One must never surrender to unhappiness, even when cancer overshadows one's life. Many joys are possible in marriage or in any loving relationship despite the struggles and challenges that exist.

Some say it takes a lifetime to learn how to love wholeheartedly and well. When feelings are hurt or our partners fail in love, most are tempted to withdraw and leave frustration behind. Intimacy is a two-edged sword. True intimacy means sharing and committing to each other emotionally, spiritually, mentally and sexually. Divine Love, given by God, is the ultimate mystery and the ultimate blessing. There is no better way to learn how to love one another than to join together in prayer. For many cancer patients, the most concerning questions often are "How will my partner react to me?", "Will I still be lovable to my partner" and "Can our relationship survive despite this illness and its side effects?" But true love is directed only partially toward the body of the beloved. The human body is part of God's beautiful creation. The spiritual connection that two people share forms a strong bond of unity that no person can break -- not even death can destroy this connection.

A love that only cares about physical appearance is a love that is veiled. Our physical state can change, but our spiritual core does not. That is why true love can outlast the death of the beloved; in that sense, we can understand why love is "stronger" than death. The physical existence of the beloved may be taken by death, but one's essence cannot be destroyed. Our unique human spirit is timeless and eternal – it goes beyond the realm of space and time and never vanishes.

Loving represents entering a relationship with another as a spiritual being. A close spiritual connection is the strongest bond and the ultimate attainable form of partnership. The lover is no longer only aroused in his physical being, not stirred only in his own emotionality, but moved to the depths of his spiritual core, moved by his partner's spiritual essence. Building a spiritual partnership is the most important aspect of any significant relationship, especially marriage. Sexual loving that completely accepts embodied intimacy also heals the body's sense of incompleteness and vulnerability. Sexual love invigorates, involves, and stimulates all of our senses and can bring magic to a relationship that deeply touches our soul. Sexual desire and love can even transform one's personality and spirit, because sexual passion between two people who are deeply in love helps them understand love and confirms that invisible powers exist beyond our everyday physical world. Sexual blessedness, more than any other form of human encounter, depends on true love. It depends on the capacity of spiritual openness to reach another beyond the physical, to truly nurture, love, bless, enrich, and enrapture the heart and spirit of another. The Spirit of God flows through us when we love this way. That is why infidelity, disrespect, and deceit can have no blessedness. God cannot bless something that hurts another person so deeply – it is against the very nature of God to do so.

A true relationship depends on the ability of our spirits to reach out and embrace one another. No matter what we know intellectually, our spirit needs fulfillment. Not being fulfilled creates a void and resentment. To heal, we must understand those times in our lives when we felt rejected or deprived of affection. To protect ourselves, we learned to avoid and resent people who hurt us this way – however, we must learn to forgive and to transcend those feelings to heal and to truly love again.

A person in love finds that everything, all the everyday occurrences in life, have a purpose – a teleology that suddenly makes life explicable. The famous poet Conrad Aiken expressed that his beloved gave new meaning and purpose to his life. He described his personal transformation like Lazarus rising from the dead. His inner beauty and essence suddenly came alive (Killorin J, 1978). Writers and poets have compared love to religion because it is enlightenment, it can enrapture and transform us. Love is reviving and energizing and uplifting, so that one can fully experience the beauty, wonder, and mystery of life – what a great gift! Finding words that truly express our deepest feelings and experiences, demonstrate our affection, and even express our fears and concerns is fulfilling. It touches us deeper than the heart, it reaches us at the soul level. Expressing love with the simplicity of emotion and elegance of language can be very seductive and can make a relationship and a life together immeasurably richer (Davidson CN, 1996)..

In a spiritual relationship, the sexual union is almost sacred; God is present and also glorified. Without the spiritual depth and bond that two lovers share, the diagnosis of cancer, surgery, and other treatments would be difficult to endure. When the physical body fails, the spirit will sustain, even in the most difficult of times. That is why the practices of prayer, meditation, and faith are so important – those practices can open us to the miracle and power of Divine Love. But unless we put Divine Love into human practice, we have missed the point. Ultimately an intimate relationship is one of the most powerful pathways to God because it is guided by the heart. Following the path of the heart requires surrendering to God – and surrendering does not mean giving up, but yielding to a much greater Power (Sandford J, Sandford P, 1985).

No one I know has been more poignant than Dr. Victor Frankl, who wrote much about the meaning of life and suffering. Love is not deserved, it is unmerited -- it is simple grace. "But love is not only grace; it is also enchantment. For the lover, it casts a spell upon the world, envelops the world in added worth. Love enormously increases receptivity and awareness to the fullness of values. The gates to the whole universe of values are, as it were, thrown wide open. Thus, in his surrender to the other, the lover experiences an inner enrichment which goes beyond anything he has ever experienced; for him the whole cosmos broadens and deepens in worth, glows in radiance of those values which only the lover sees. For it is well known that love does not make one blind but seeing – able to see values, meaning, able to see the hand of God" (Frankl VE, 1980).

This deep spiritual love can endure any trial, illness and even death. When two people love like this, their love gives the deepest meaning to life – there is no greater purpose in life than love. Cancer should never destroy a relationship; in fact, it can enhance and deepen the love two people have for each other. A marriage or relationship in which heart speaks to heart is a gift from God, and no gift that comes from God is temporary or coincidental. All that comes from God participates in eternal life. Love between two people, when given by God, is stronger than death. When we have loved deeply, that love can grow even stronger after the death of the person we love.

One powerful and healing way to express deep love is through sexual affection. Many patients with cancer express feeling uneasy, uncomfortable and even ashamed of resuming sexual intimacy after cancer surgery or treatment. Partners are often confused and hesitant to initiate sexual affection. Part of our spirituality is the ability to experience sexual affection and pleasure with our partners. God designed our bodies and spirits to enjoy sex. He united our sensitive spirits with our intricate, wonderfully strong, feeling bodies to give us great heights and joy in sexual union. Sexual energy is a life force that permeates all of creation and is part of the joyfulness of life creation. It is important to realize that the human capacity for ecstasy is a normal part of who we are and is a God-given gift that provides healing energy to the body, mind and spirit (Moore T, 1994). Avoiding affectionate touch, physical closeness, or sexual intimacy deprives one's soul of the essence to heal. One who refrains from sexual intimacy gives a very hurtful message to his partner suffering from cancer.

Any form of sexual avoidance or rejection can feel devastating, especially to one with cancer. Sex creates a union between partners and is an avenue of expression, a means of making a statement about our comfort in relating physically to our partner. Sexual union, for all its physical pleasures, also symbolizes a spiritual union, forming a transcendent bond between two loving people. Love is life energy at its purest form and is so powerful that it literally holds together every cell in our being. It is the glue that unites us. Sexual blessedness, more than any other form of human encounter, has the capacity to nurture, bless, enrich, energize and enrapture the heart and spirit of another. Love is the threshold which moves us beyond fear and shame. When we are devoid of love, we feel fear, doubt, and confusion – and are exposed to many other negative emotions and feelings. God gives us love, peace and joy, which impart hope, faith and optimism. This is perhaps God's greatest gift to mankind.

It is important for partners to discuss any physical or sexual concerns with their doctor. It is devastating, lonely and hurtful for a partner to be avoided sexually because of cancer. Emotionally, this is extremely stressful and places one in a state of abandonment and rejection. When we are comforted by another, we feel a sense of belonging and connection to God in the highest and most sacred aspect of our being. If God dwells within us, we will never be alone. God provides to the lonely what the world cannot give. He places us into the hands of loving, compassionate people. God provides us with the one friend or companion who is chosen by Him to touch our heart in ways we have not been touched before – and just at the time we need it the most.

Many patients with cancer have spoken of their illness as a "wake up call." They are awaking to experience life in a different way, with increased awareness. It is important to bless each morning, to wake up and thank God for friends and family. Many patients who have been diagnosed with cancer have learned that it is time to return to God and to remember that there is light beyond the darkness. There is an opportunity to grow and to truly transform our spirit. Had we died three weeks ago with a sudden heart attack, the opportunity for spiritual growth and expressing our love to the people we so deeply appreciate would be lost. Now, the opportunity is before us – our spirit can progress along its journey. The more time we spend communicating with God in our thoughts, our prayers, and our actions, the greater is our capacity to develop and nurture love. Spiritual transformation is not about becoming more complicated or sensitive – instead, it is about simplifying our thoughts, our behavior, and our life. Spiritual growth allows us to love more deeply, to express our love more openly, and to show our love in action. The purpose of a holy relationship is to heal, not to hurt.

Healing cannot occur when our wounds are hidden or repressed. Healing occurs when our wounds are exposed to light. Only the truth can heal. When we heal, we see life and the world through different eyes. We begin observing many little details in a way that we had not done for years. We see beauty, we see wonder, we experience meaning, we are alive again – this can happen even if our physical body is damaged or ill. The greatest and deepest regret so many people fear is the regret of never having expressed their true feelings of affection to a loved one. When the sudden death of one's mother or father occurs, we are saddened by the thought that we did not have the opportunity to tell them how much they really meant to us. It is important to express forgiveness, appreciation, gratitude, and blessing – a beautiful letter can be composed. It sets the reader, the beloved, free from guilt and the letter will never lose its power. In fact, with time, this letter will be even more powerful and meaningful.

Writing such a letter will release a positive, invigorating energy throughout your body and can be extremely healing for you and your beloved. Our body, our mind, and our spirit will respond as there is no other energy as strong, as healing, or as transforming as the power of love. That is why God in his wisdom has saved us, because we love and love covers a multitude of sins. It is love that connects us beyond the realm of death, love is immortal. Love is the one thing that God really asks of us, and only love has the power to save us – without it, we are lost. Our life's most important purpose is growth of our spirit and transformation of our soul.

Perfect health is not the goal of healing -- love, peace, and joy are the ultimate goals, independent of our physical health, finances, and other worldly possessions. Healing does not necessarily mean the remission or cure of cancer. The most significant healing happens deep inside the human spirit. The ultimate healing and transformation of the spirit occurs with death itself. That is why we have nothing to fear and if we can learn to grow spiritually while we are still here on this earth, we have a wonderful opportunity to serve others and to help them heal. Life is meant to be meaningful, and if the only way to find meaning is in our pain, then suffering is a gift. God never promised that we will not suffer; in fact, He said, "blessed are the ones who suffer" and He promised to give us the strength and ability to cope with our suffering.

Sister Rose has had several life-threatening cancer surgeries and said that she never believed that her cancer was a punishment. She knew deep within her spirit that God's love would be affirmed in the depths of her suffering. He was her strength when her body seemed too weak to hold onto life. If we learn only one lesson on this journey, we need to learn how important it is to love and to give of ourselves. We must send love to our mind, our body, and to others. Ask the Spirit of God for three minutes to touch the heart of a friend or a relative and visualize that person being illuminated in God's divine light. These short prayers have tremendous power and place the person we pray for in immediate connection to the divine – especially when we pray for healing or to give someone strength or to send our love to them.

We can ask God for specific signs at any time. God communicates to us through our friends, loved ones, dreams, visions, and especially nature. All we need to do is to ask – as the saying goes, seek and you will find, ask and you will be given, and knock and the door will open. It always works. God is amazing, one thought and we are connected to Him who rules the universe. Prayer is extremely powerful. Thinking about God, giving to others is prayer. Our work can become our prayer. Whenever I see a new patient, I pray especially to their guardian angel for insight and direction. Analyzing the human mind is a complex process, often more difficult then diagnosing a cancerous growth. The mind is endlessly complex and unpredictable, but the greatest pain is often within one's spirit – and that is why I pray for divine help, so I can sense when a spirit is broken. A broken spirit, can only be healed by God and He can use us as instruments of healing if we are willing.

I will never forget many years ago when a young woman came to see me. She was 24 years old and suffered from episodic depression for years. During the initial interview, I was compelled to ask if she believed in God. I usually don't ask that question in a clinical interview and she looked at me in amazement and she said, "Why do you ask me, do you?" I told her that I do believe in God and I do believe in His Love and mercy and most of all in the concept of eternal life. She started to challenge me and I regretted ever approaching the subject. But somehow I could sense that she was touched. After our session she made a follow-up appointment but never came back. I was afraid that I had contributed to her discomfort and that she would not return to see me again. I regretted at that moment my questioning her belief in God. Later that day, the nurse told me that she never canceled her appointment. I asked my nurse to give her a call at home and to leave a message. I wanted to make sure that she was alright. Two days later we received a phone call from her sister who informed us that Debbie died in a car accident the day after she came to see me. Deeply shocked by the news I realized that our meeting was no coincidence. I knew she was with God and I also knew that our conversation about God, faith, and life was not a mistake, but divine intervention. I went to my office and reviewed my notes on her visit – I realized that I ended with a note to myself that read, "Why did I do this?" We sometimes have only one opportunity to touch a person's soul, and it is important to take that chance – if we do, we can never go wrong.

When we pray for a patient to be in the hands of God, it is a comforting belief, but it is most of all a reality. Prayer is asking God for help. A spiritual crisis is not a deterioration of faith, but a loss of trust in God, ourself, and others. Distrust can throw us into a psychological struggle, but that struggle can also help us to evolve spiritually. We must learn to take delight in life and to become life affirming rather than hopeless and fearful. The search for our spiritual essence is not an escape from life, but the reverse – it is a profound level of commitment to participate in our own creation, in living in our spirit that transcends illness, such as cancer. Spirituality gives us the strength to cope with all of life's struggles, but we must be open to learning, growing, and progressing on our spiritual journey.

With every relationship that heals, we bring love, light, and peace into the world. To experience that kind of love is a gift from God for which we must be thankful. The purpose of spiritual growth is to awaken to our real self and to find our spiritual essence. In a spiritual relationship, people should be free as individuals, while being united with each other through the love of God. This type of relationship is one of the most powerful pathways to God, because it begins with the heart. The purpose of God is to unite. A relationship, a teaching or a religion that divides is not of God, but manmade. We must all learn from one another and the ultimate goal is to become better human beings who are more loving, more compassionate and more giving.

The spiritual life is typically not a conscious choice, but often happens in the midst of a challenging and difficult life event. We need to look closely at the way we think, communicate, interact, and feel in order to become more aware of our spiritual nature. A spiritual life requires discipline to listen to God, who constantly communicates with us, but whom we seldom hear. When we learn to listen to that quiet and gentle inner voice, we become more aware of the true purpose of our lives. Consider the following questions for a few moments. Be honest and fair as you answer these questions about yourself, your motives and values in life, and how you treat your loved ones. It is time to transform your spirit, awaken your soul and progress on that spiritual journey!

Questions for self- examination and reflection:

1. Are you empathetic and compassionate towards others?
2. Do you feel with and for others?
3. Would you consider yourself a passionate person?
4. Do you offer friendship and kindness to others?
5. Would you consider yourself thoughtful?

6. Do you have a warm and loving personality?

7. Are you forgiving?

8. Are you sincere with others?

9. Are you encouraging and appreciative?

10. Can you see the Good in others?

11. Are you dedicated and supportive of others?

12. Do you bring out the best in people?

13. Can you be nurturing, giving and generous?

14. Do you consider yourself truly loving?

15. Do you feel privileged to be in the life of others?

16. Can you openly express you feelings and love to your partner, or are you holding back?

Love is difficult to define as it can mean different things to different people. Genuine love desires the best for the other person, even if that means withdrawing from other's life. Love wants the other person to become strong, healthy, and independent and respects one's individuality. Love does not claim the other person for possession or control. A true lover gives unconditionally with no restrictions and no expectations in return. The attitude is that good is to be done, no matter who receives the credit. There are no hidden self-interests or agendas. Actions and intensions are directed only toward the good of another, without one's own needs being considered. Genuine love increases through giving and becomes a source of overflowing joy. People who can truly love this way are among the most radiant human beings one can hope to find; they touch the hearts and souls of almost everyone. One of the most important forms of their generosity is their generosity of spirit. They have healthy ways of expressing their love to others. Without trying to do so, people who are truly loving have a tremendous effect on others.

They can be stimulating and naturally seductive without wanting or trying to do so. One would think that people like this can be taken for granted but quite the opposite is true. Love enables you to have strong boundaries and good morals because the motivation is not self-seeking or manipulative – it is so genuine that they are able to withdraw when necessary. They have a desire to love, not a need to be loved.

True love, Divine Love, helps us to heal and to heal others. It gives us emotional power, physical strength, and our spiritual essence. The ability to live and to love in this way is truly a sacred gift. We must learn to treasure our spiritual strength as well as the people and relationships encountered along the course of our spiritual journey. The **spirit to heal** is deep within each one of us!

CHAPTER 9

THE HEALING SPIRIT

"The prayer of faith shall save the sick"

New Testament: James 5:15

Depression and anxiety are common among patients who suffer from chronic illness, such as cancer. These symptoms often begin as part of the initial traumatic response, when one is still in shock and unable to completely comprehend what is happening. During these difficult times, many patients experience feelings of hopelessness, despair, anxiety, and a spiritual brokenness and emptiness that can be hard to explain. These spiritual responses are difficult to treat, and medication, therapy and support groups provide little help. Traditional psychiatry provides us with insight into these problems but has difficulty healing emotional issues rooted in the human soul. God can empower and heal us beyond the limits of knowledge and medicine – He has direct access our heart and spirit.

The healing of cancer patients can benefit from both medical therapy to combat the physical disease and a spiritual integrated approach to deal with the emotional stress and suffering. Combining these two treatment approaches is powerful and perhaps one of the most beautiful ways to experience the love of God. We may not understand the scientific basis of spiritual healing, but we can only benefit from opening ourselves to the mysterious healing of God's love.

Over the past decade, several therapies have shown variable degrees of success in relieving the symptoms of depression and anxiety. For example, cognitive therapies alleviate depression and anxiety by helping people change their negative thinking patterns; interpersonal therapies provide relief by helping patients resolve relationship difficulties; anti-depressant medications can treat depressed mood, fatigue, concentration difficulties, insomnia, and other physical symptoms that accompany anxiety and depression. Although these therapies and medications can relieve depression to some extent, none effectively treats problems of a spiritual nature. The inability of conventional therapies to treat spiritual problems is concerning for several important reasons. First, the standard techniques are ineffective in treating at least one third of patients – leaving many with symptoms which can impair their quality of life. Second, one's spiritual brokenness or religious concerns can aggravate conventional causes of depression and anxiety. Third, intense spiritual problems can directly cause symptoms, adding to those already present from the diagnosis and treatment of cancer. Patients often feel unable to gain insight, to experience personal growth, or to find peace without turning to spirituality. Instead, they can become fixed in a state of persistent anxiety, fear and concern. Dr. Albert Schweitzer once stated that one of the great human tragedies is what dies inside of us while we still live (Cousins N, 1996). We must not let that happen to our spirit!

The purely secular approach of conventional medicine tends to ignore or diminish spiritual concerns, an attitude which can compromise one's recovery. Even with medication and conventional therapy, patients experience an emotional numbness and often do not express their emotional and psychological feelings. Emotional numbness inhibits healing and recovery from the trauma of illness. Patients with this mindset find it much more difficult to cope with the many challenges of a disease like cancer. Without hope and faith, our internal world becomes weak and can permanently change how we deal with stress and our life crises. Our mind, body and spirit are designed for optimal survival during difficult times. The human spirit is strong enough to sustain us when our body, mind and emotional strength are depleted. Cancer confronts us with the challenge to examine our lives, to re-evaluate who we are, and to determine our own personal goals for the future.

During cancer treatment, many patients express a sense of abandonment by God or feel unworthy of His love. These beliefs can foster intense hopelessness and despair. Spiritual hopelessness and depression create a deeper pain and despair than that usually seen in depressed patients without spiritual involvement – this is especially true when combined with the trauma of cancer. To restore one's emotional, physical, and spiritual well-being and to regain hope for healing, one must change negative patterns of thinking and feelings toward God. With Spiritual Integrated Therapy, one can strengthen his connection to the love of God.

We believe that Spiritual Integrated Therapy has tremendous potential. Not only can this type of therapy relieve spiritual depression, it can also enhance self-awareness, facilitate spiritual growth and transformation, and provide a greater meaning to one's life. The spiritual integrated approach can help people appreciate their own uniqueness and to accept their suffering as an opportunity for spiritual growth. Patients with cancer can learn to appreciate every moment and to live in that moment without fear of the future. Because spiritually based therapies emphasize the importance of forgiveness, surrender, love, compassion and acceptance, they can improve relationships as individuals seek peace within themselves and others. The treatment approach that we have developed can bridge the gap between traditional psychotherapy and spiritual therapy. The spiritual integrated treatment approach addresses not only spiritual issues but also invites God into the process of healing. Spiritual psychotherapy brings a divine perspective into feelings deep within our soul. Our spiritual connection to God is essential for healing of our damaged and fragile emotions. The goals of this therapy are to alleviate depression and fear and to strengthen our relationship with God.

Patients often ask how the spiritual approach can make a difference. The depression that accompanies the diagnosis of cancer or illness is different than typical depression or common mood disorders. Hopelessness, despair, and the fear of being abandoned by God contribute to a loss of faith, or a spiritual crisis, and can lead to a separation from the divine love of God. The spiritual approach specifically addresses all of these areas – it is a journey that awakens us to God's love and recognizes our intrinsic worth as a human being. By experiencing God's love, we find a sense of peace that does not depend on our own resources. Knowing the reality of His love is important, especially in times of a life crisis such as cancer. By establishing trust that God will provide us with strength, no matter how difficult our situation may be, we are provided with tremendous healing power. Being able to surrender to God can reduce our anxiety and relieve our despair. In times of suffering, our faith in God reduces our need to rely on others; we become stronger, more independent, and start to undergo personal growth and transformation of our spirit.

The spiritual integrated approach can significantly affect many types of situations that previously aroused fear, anxiety or depression. One may find that he experiences less disappointment, anger, and despair than ever before. Some patients have even reported new feelings of well-being and contentment and a greater ability to cope with physical pain and suffering despite their illness. And most of all, they have learned to trust God and to understand more fully the eternal and spiritual perspective of life. Spiritual therapy helps one cope with present life difficulties and future fears by utilizing spiritual and religious resources.

The initial focus of treatment is determined largely by a clinical assessment evaluation, a life history that focuses on spiritual concerns and problems. This assessment is specifically designed to access those spiritual problems and experiences that might have distorted one's image of God; it also examines forgiveness, love, and the meaning and purpose of one's life. It is important to reveal instances when one felt like he could no longer go on living. These situations obviously represent intense life experiences which must be resolved in order to achieve peace and healing.

The patient is met wherever he is at that moment so that his unique needs, concerns, and symptoms are the main focus of therapy. How one thinks of oneself and evaluates self worth is important and is independent of achievements, education or professional status. One must examine his spiritual beliefs and religious practice and, if such beliefs are dysfunctional, can begin the process of reconstructing and healing. Going back into our life's journey, we must release hidden or forgotten resentments, hostile feelings and times of unforgiveness. We must work through spiritual doubts, confusion and concerns and learn to enhance our ability to give and to receive love, both interpersonally and with God. We will begin to feel peace, joy, gratitude and many other positive emotions and limit feelings of anxiety and fear. We will learn to unload stress and anxiety-producing thoughts through the use of prayer-imagery, healing meditations and other spiritual techniques. And most of all, we will discover greater meaning in the experiences of our life and will expand our faith, hope and ability to trust God and others.

Many cancer patients and those in other difficult situations find it hard to pray, especially for themselves. Feelings of abandonment, that God might be absent at this time of great distress, are emotionally very debilitating and painful. At that time one can feel disconnected from the love of God – this feeling is often expressed as disappointment of an unheard prayer to God. Sometimes it seems easier not to pray at all, and since prayer is our communication to God, not praying disrupts our divine connection. But, we don't need words in order to pray – our tears and the pain we feel is one of the deepest forms of prayer. At times we may even wonder where God is. In His infinite compassion, the following parable by Gerald Heard called "Dryness and the Dark Night" may help us understand this concept (Keating T, 1996):

One scientist devoted his life to developing a strain of butterfly that would be the most beautiful combination of colors ever seen on this planet. After years of study and experiment-ation he was certain that he had a cocoon that would produce his genetic masterpiece. On the day the butterfly was expected to emerge, he gathered his entire staff together. All waited breathlessly as the creature began to work its way out of the cocoon. It disengaged its right wing, its body, and most of its left wing. Just as the staff was ready to cheer and celebrate this event, they saw with horror that the tip of the left wing of the butterfly was stuck in the mouth of the cocoon. The creature was desperately flapping its other wing to free itself. As it labored, it grew more and more exhausted. Each new effort seemed more difficult, and the intervals between efforts grew longer and longer. At last the scientist, unable to bear the tension of this struggle, took a scalpel and cut a tiny section from the mouth of the cocoon. With one final burst of strength the butterfly fell free onto the laboratory table. Everyone cheered with excitement. Then silence again descended on the room. Although the butterfly was free, it could not fly. The struggle to escape from the cocoon is nature's way of forcing blood to the edges of the butterfly's wings so that, upon emerging, it can enjoy its new life and fly to its heart content. In seeking to save the butterfly's life, the scientist had truncated its capacity to function. A butterfly that cannot fly is a contradiction in terms. This is a mistake God does not make. God holds back his infinite mercy from rushing to the rescue when we are struggling or challenged. He will not actively intervene because our struggle strengthens our spirit and prepares every recess of our being for the divine energy of grace.

How often have we wondered where God was in our difficult or painful times? Only when we look back and can reflect on these times at a distance can we clearly see that God was there all the time. Being diagnosed with cancer can make one question his faith, religion and God. Where is God? We may wonder if we are being punished for something we have done in the past. Is all this a sign that we are not loved by God? These negative spiritual beliefs deplete us of our spiritual energy and strength and may cause us to feel crushed, broken, empty or even emotionally dead. During these times it is difficult to feel the mercy and love of God – we might even feel that we are not deserving of God's love. How can we resolve these feelings?

Let's consider the spiritual crisis and abandonment felt by Myra, a woman who was diagnosed with breast cancer shortly after the death of her husband. She felt so terribly crushed and alone at that time and was convinced that God had abandoned her and that she could never trust Him again. She withdrew from life and from her children and became more and more depressed. The depression was not triggered by the diagnosis itself but by her perception and negative beliefs towards God. Myra slipped into a crisis of faith, and she was unable to believe or trust in the goodness of God. Everything Myra believed as a child about loving God was suddenly in question, and she found herself in a deep dark hole from she could not escape. Myra was unable to make important decisions about her cancer treatment and a good friend convinced her to see a therapist to deal with her spiritual crisis and loss of faith. Myra began to see the emptiness inside her soul and realized that it was she who had abandoned God. God did not abandon her – He never abandons anyone. Since the death of her husband, she felt that life was empty, and she almost wished she could die too. Her children, her friends and her co-workers had noticed for months that Myra had given up on life – they felt that she had slipped into depression. Being diagnosed with breast cancer caused Myra to realize that she really wanted to live. Now she knew that, in order to survive, she must adopt a hopeful attitude for herself and others around her. After several months of therapy, Myra realized that the diagnosis of cancer had not destroyed her life at all. The opposite was true, the diagnosis of breast cancer gave Myra new purpose and a renewed will to live. She needed to learn to trust God again and most of all to feel loved by Him. Examining her own spiritual and religious beliefs was an important step in beginning the process of healing.

We all develop a series of defense mechanisms to deny, avoid or lessen emotional pain. Sometimes it is easier to forget the painful past and to move ahead with our life rather than allowing the Spirit of God to search the innermost parts of our heart and soul to achieve true healing. Forgiveness lies at the very heart of healing, and we cannot heal without forgiveness. We need to forgive in order to be forgiven.

Forgiveness is God's gift to us, the gift of His grace. It is necessary to rely on God's help when forgiveness seems impossible. This is not an intellectual decision alone but an act of God's grace, in union with our spirit. In our human frailty, it is hard to forgive the seemingly unforgivable. However, by inviting God's love and allowing Him to work within us, we can transcend our human limitations and extend forgiveness to those who have hurt us. Forgiveness enables us to let go of the past and gain emotional strength – it releases negative energy that may have been stored in our body for months or years. God has designed us to love, and we require love to survive and heal. When we act resentful or unloving or harbor hostile emotions toward others and ourselves, we disturb our physical, emotional and spiritual balance. We all have experienced the negative energy that resonates from someone who is angry and resentful – we sense unpleasantness, uneasiness and sometimes outright hostility. Our body, mind and spirit naturally strive for harmony, love, and tranquility. For the same reasons, we respond to the compassionate and loving person in a positive way. It gives us strength and vitality, where negative responses cause tension, hurt and sadness. These energies play a very significant role in our overall health. In order to heal we need to access our positive energies and relinquish our negative ones. Holding onto hurtful experiences and harboring resentment and unforgiveness damages our well being and blocks the healing process. When we are held back by painful experiences of the past, we interfere with the natural flow of life and impair healing. Healing requires release of these emotional burdens. Forgiveness helps us to move from that pain into the healing love of God. Forgiveness releases us from negative and destructive energy and is cleansing to our hearts and souls. Any therapy that does not involve the process of true forgiveness cannot help us heal spiritually.

Spiritual wounds are much deeper and more painful than any other hurt because they strike at the innermost core of our being. These wounds, if not healed, create a sensitivity and vulnerability within us and affect our feelings, thoughts and actions throughout life. God can only move within us and heal us when we invite Him into our life. Jane, a 43-year-old patient, felt devastated after being diagnosed with breast cancer. After successful lumpectomy surgery and radiation therapy, her chances for survival were 90 percent; but, Jane was depressed. She felt the deep spiritual agony of being abandoned, punished and totally rejected by God. Jane blamed God for her cancer, and she was angry that all her years of trying to do the right thing, going to church and praying had not prevented this disease. She was unable to find peace even when her doctor had reassured her of excellent recovery and prognosis. Jane lost trust in the God she once loved. At the root of these feelings were past episodes of rejection and abandonment. Specifically, Jane grew up with a harsh and critical father who did not understand when she would cry. He would talk to her only after she stopped crying, and she felt rejected and alone. She felt that her father's love was conditional to her behavior. Many people grew up with criticism although some have experienced it much more intensely than others.

Regardless if the criticism came from our parents, teachers, or friends, it can hurt us deeply. Our response, whether expressed or repressed, was anger. As children, we view God dressed in the attitudes and behavior of our parents or caregivers. Our picture of God can become distorted, and we then fail to see God as a loving and caring Presence. When we learn as children that love is conditional, it clouds our image of God. These past experiences can prevent us from seeing God in the most important light of all – that of unconditional love.

Negative religious experiences can also induce guilt, shame or inferiority and hurt us deeply. The loss of a loved one through death or abandonment can distance us from God. Making sense out of human suffering, such as cancer, can leave us feeling alone and rejected by God. Rational understanding of circumstances cannot heal our soul and heart. Only God can restore our spiritual brokenness and help us overcome these wounds – and it is not until we forgive others who have hurt us, that we can see God as loving and kind. In order to heal, we need to believe in a God of love, forgiveness, and mercy. We must come to peace first in the most important relationship of all, our relationship with God. Even for a profoundly devoted person like our Sister Rose, who never once doubted the love and healing power of God, her world came crashing down. In times like this, it is difficult to maintain our faith. Many devoted people have known desolation and lacked awareness of God's presence in the midst of suffering, simply because their flow of life had been interrupted. But remember, God does not abandon us in our pain and despair. He is right there with us, inviting us to explore the depths of our being so that we can heal more fully and deeply.

Our future is uncertain whether we face illness or not, and peace can only be found by surrendering all aspects of our lives into the hands of God. That is why the most important aspect of our spiritual healing is to learn to trust God in difficult times and to surrender our pain and fear to Him. The process of inner healing begins by acknowledging our deepest moments of despair or fear and surrendering them to God. We need to be attentive to those areas of our life to experience freedom from fear and hopelessness. Doubting the goodness and the love of God can be more painful and agonizing than our physical illness and can lead to a crisis of faith and hopelessness. If we do not believe that God loves us, we will find it difficult to experience love and trust in others. Inner healing requires that we restore and heal our relationship with God, to experience His love and goodness. With our willingness to reflect upon the innermost parts of our soul, we set our healing process in motion. We must find peace and union with God so that our sprit can experience peace.

Spiritual Integrated Therapy is not based on a particular method or technique because every individual is unique. This type of therapy consists of surrendering one's heart, mind, and soul to God. Under the guidance of the Spirit of God, one's pain is released to God in prayer. Healing occurs with transformation of the heart, mind, soul, and spirit and can have a positive outcome on our physical health. Transformation occurs when God turns our burden to glory, our weakness to strength, and our despair to hope. Transformation often follows after we have experienced spiritual brokenness or face a crisis in our life. Many people think of healing in association with physical health but the greatest, deepest and most profound healing is that of the human spirit.

Why does our spirit need healing? We are quick to blame God when things have gone wrong and often forget that we are responsible for our own choices. We must examine ourselves from a deep spiritual level and invite God to meet us at that level of our being. No pain is sharper than the feeling of being abandoned by God – yet, many times that is one of our first reactions when we are faced with a life crisis. Patients frequently express their emotional pain as feeling crushed spiritually. The Apostles felt the same despair and desolation at times, even though they physically walked with Jesus. Their agony but also their hope and relief was expressed in their writings and psalms: "The Lord is near to the broken hearted, and saves those who are crushed in Spirit" (Ps 34:18). "Where once we felt broken and crushed, we now feel blessed. Strength is made perfect in weakness" (2 Cor.12:9).

Healing does not mean that we have forgotten or erased the painful past – that would defeat the purpose of living through hurtful events. Healing occurs when we shift from resentment to forgiveness, from judgment to acceptance, from fear to trust, from despair to hope, and most of all when we choose to love. Only God can perform this deep spiritual healing. We must permit God to heal our pain as He desires to heal, to forgive, to provide joy and peace, and to release us from pain. We must give God permission to heal us and to touch these wounded places with His love. When our pain has been inflicted by another person, we have to ask God to forgive that person and to help us to do the same. This form of therapy heals not only our emotional and psychological state, but also treats the depths of our spirit and soul. Increasingly the problems for which people seek help involve religious and spiritual issues.

Patients seek to share their beliefs and look for divine support in difficult life situations. Traditional psychotherapy helps us to understand the weak and vulnerable moments in our life and the way we respond to them. Often we react by expressing anger or by withdrawing from those situations. Releasing emotions by expressing our feelings is important but that alone does not heal our deep pain. Everyone has painful memories from the past which need to be released, even if they seem unimportant. Tim, a 49-year-old engineer recalls an incident in his past many of us may have experienced in one way or another. He was 11 years old when asked by his teacher to solve a math problem on the blackboard in front of his entire class. Tim knew why he was chosen by his teacher because he was distracted and not paying attention. When Tim failed to solve the problem, the teacher and his entire class started to make fun of him. He remembered this incident and suffered from social anxiety and low self esteem in school; later in adulthood, he developed performance anxiety which hindered him at work. Not everyone would have had the same devastating effects from this experience, but Tim was very sensitive to criticism and took this experience to heart. In a healing prayer-imagery Tim surrendered this situation to God, including the feelings of anger and resentment he felt for so many years. Through this prayer-imagery, he was finally able to forgive his teacher. Many of us have suffered similar trauma in the past – the hurt can stay with us for years and is not healed until it is released emotionally, mentally, and spiritually. Even some physical responses to emotional problems can be released with healing prayer. People with irritable bowel syndrome, colitis, high blood pressure or a weak immune system can experience reduction or relief of symptoms when true inner healing occurs in the heart and spirit.

The deepest type of wounding occurs when children are deprived of love and unconditional acceptance. The basic need of life is love; being deprived of love impairs our ability to love and trust others and can affect us deep within our spirit. When we experience fear, anxiety or resentment, or are unable to love or to trust, we need healing. The Spirit of God is able to reach the inner, most vulnerable parts of our being to help us heal – God is able to do what we as human beings cannot.

One of the most touching examples of healing a wounded spirit is the story of little Anna who was brought to me by her parents when she was four years old. She suffered from recurrent nightmares, weight loss, and respiratory infections, and was listless and unable to speak. Anna was adopted by her parents; she was the oldest of four siblings. Her natural parents gave the children up for adoption because of extreme poverty. Each year one of her siblings was adopted from the orphanage, only Anna and her twin brother were left. When Anna was chosen for adoption, she was separated from her brother, sent on a 15-hour train ride to meet her new parents, and then went by plane to her new home in another country. Anna ate very little, she did not smile, and she did not appear to enjoy anything – her parents provided her with everything they could but nothing changed. Anna quietly cried during the night and started screaming when her parents tried to rock her back to sleep. Her parents contacted a child psychologist who tested the child extensively. After a series of psychological and developmental tests and therapy, Anna showed no signs of improvement. Another doctor suspected possible brain damage by malnutrition that Anna experienced early in life, so she was tested again. She was given little hope to improve. The problem was more than developmental and psychological, it was spiritual. Anna's heart was broken, all she had experienced in her young life was one rejection and one loss after another. It was too much to bear and this was her way of emotionally shutting down. When I saw Anna at age five, she was so tiny and petite that she looked like a two-year-old. She suffered from severe childhood depression, separation anxiety, stomach cramps, colitis and total body rash. She was listless, glassy eyed and unresponsive. Deep within Anna's spirit was an overwhelming anxiety; as young as she was, she never experienced the peace of feeling secure, safe and loved. By the time she was adopted she had developed a defense mechanism to protect herself from emotional pain. She emotionally withdrew from everyone around her, causing her to build up great anxiety and distress. Her parents came to see me in total despair – they loved Anna so much and provided everything for her but did not know how to help her. Anna spoke very little but I felt she could understand more than she could speak. I gave Anna's parents a prayer and asked them to pray over Anna every night. After several weeks, Anna began sleeping through the night without awakening, her nightmares were gone. This is the prayer Anna's parents spoke over her every night.

> Anna, you are a child of God, you are chosen and precious. God and we love you because of whom you are. God has created you and has called you into our life. You are not a replacement for anyone, you are unique and special. God, we know that You are delighted with Anna

and You created her out of Your own heart
of love. This one, Lord, is chosen and
precious, a treasure to You and a blessing
to us. Please pour Your healing light and
love into Anna's spirit until all wounds are
healed, all fears and anxieties are calmed.
Hold Anna, Lord, in Your loving arms
tonight and surround her with angels as she
sleeps. Let her feel secure and safe
surrounded by Your love. – AMEN
(Sandford J, Sandford P, 1885)

The prayers were not only for strengthening her little
body, but especially for healing her wounded spirit. Anna's spirit
needed nurture and love through deep inner healing prayer. It was
not long before Anna began to respond with a new alertness to
her environment. Anna's heart opened naturally in response to
the tenderness, warmth and love that was communicated through
her parents' prayers. The miracle of love is that Anna is a
survivor of circumstances that would have killed many others.
Her spirit needed healing, and we could see Anna being
transformed through the miracle of love, God's love. She began
to smile, to interact with other children, and finally to talk in
almost perfect English. What was astonishing to all of us is that
Anna could recite the prayer that was spoken over her while she
slept. Anna began to amaze us more and more – she is a perfect
example of divine inner healing, a child traditional psychology
could not help.

Inner healing is divine therapy and a powerful way to heal;
the basic goal is to connect people with the strength and healing
love of God and to invite Him into the healing process. Life

experiences can be overwhelming. Unless we have faith in the divine power of God and are able to draw upon God's strength during these difficult times, certain life situations can be almost unbearable. Life confronts us abruptly with a challenge, it may be a tragedy, loss or illness, over which we have little or no control. The inner healing of Spiritually Integrated Therapy facilitates personal growth, establishes meaning for one's life and draws upon divine wisdom at times when there is no other answer. It provides us with a spiritual anchor or lifeline we can depend on regardless of our circumstances. This therapy seeks to mobilize one's resources to cope with the most severe life crises. All healing forces are God-given and need to be released by that person in order to effect healing. Only when we are able to experience God's love, which is often brought to us through others, can healing of our spirit and emotions occur.

Forgiveness lies at the heart of inner healing, and each challenge we encounter is an opportunity for forgiveness. But forgiveness is a process, not a one time event – it takes heartfelt compassion, love, and the surrender of pride, control, and judgment to achieve total forgiveness. This process involves God's grace and mercy and becomes a significant healing factor.

Often hope, like faith, is found in darkness. Hope is part of healing, and we can explore and uncover the essence of our own unique spirit with healing. We discover our inner core layer by layer, just like peeling an onion. After all the layers have been removed, a shiny white core is exposed that is without any cover. That core represents our inner and most vulnerable being. Willingness and awareness are the keys to uncovering our inner core. We can succeed in healing our spirit if we are willing to uncover our true essence and surrender to God – we must have hope and faith.

Truth allows us to live in reality, in the here and now – and that is precisely where God will meet us. From the present, He can walk back with us through our past experiences to strengthen and transform our spirit. We also need to be willing to discover all the ways we resist reality and change, including our perception of self image, our fears, and our ways of responding to life's challenges and losses. We do not possess the power to transform ourselves; transformation of our spirit is the divine work of the Spirit of God, which is why it is so important to communicate and connect to God through prayer. Spiritual transformation is a process, a way of life, a journey – it is not an immediate phenomenon.

The human spirit has an innate wisdom and yearns to be free – listening with our heart is essential. The heart is the seat of our emotional life, and we can only listen to our heart when our mind and heart are connected – and that is often the longest and most difficult part of our journey. Our journey of spiritual healing on earth will continue as long as live, until our last breath. We may feel uncomfortable at times, but we must persevere if we are to achieve true healing of our spirit and soul.

We must remember that we are born from God's love. He created us to be wise and noble, to be loving, kind and generous, to encourage others on their journey, to be creative, and to share our God-given talents and abilities. We must renew ourselves constantly to be engaged in the world of awe and wonder and faith. We can see beauty in a person through the eyes of our spirit. God gave us what it takes to be strong and loving, to have courage and to be joyous and accomplished. We can learn and grow from a life that presents us with many unfolding mysteries. Pain and suffering are only part of those mysteries and give us the opportunity to grow personally and to extend ourselves to others. Even in our deepest struggles, we find that we can experience peace of mind – a peace that is not created by our mind but emerges from deep within our human spirit.

With true spiritual growth and transformation, we find ourselves more alive, joyful, peaceful, and more loving. We must release resentment and negative feelings that prevent our spirit from healing. Nothing harms our spiritual tranquility more than to hold onto those feelings. When we resent another person or feel hostility toward them, we weaken our body, mind, and spirit and impair our physical health, our spirituality, and our relationship to God and others. Our reactions and attitude toward others must change if we are to achieve peace and healing. Forgiveness, faith and hope are essential for healing of our spirit. True healing must begin with return to God's love; then, life can be our greatest teacher. With every moment, every heartbeat and every breath, we have the opportunity to learn, to grow and to be loved. Our spirit must be freed of its burdens and prepared to heal through difficult times. That is when true transformation begins, when we recognize and understand our true spiritual nature. We then attain spiritual awareness. True healing can only occur through awareness, transformation and growth of our spirit.

Cancer can have devastating emotional and spiritual consequences when we succumb to fear, depression and anxiety. During these difficult times, many patients experience the pain of hopelessness, brokenness, and spiritual emptiness. Even one with strong faith can have doubts and concerns about what is happening and why it is happening – a crisis of faith can occur. This spiritual crisis takes us to a painful and lonely place where we must face our fears and re-evaluate our beliefs. At this moment, our life seems like it is shattered into hundreds or thousands of pieces – this is precisely the moment of greatest significance in our spiritual journey. Henri Nouwen once said after a beautiful crystal challis crashed onto the floor and splintered into thousands of pieces that he never knew that broken glass could shine so brightly (Nouwen HJM, 1992b). We shine in our spiritual brokenness, and it seems that others see the light in us before we do. When our world and life is suddenly shattered into pieces, remember that God's light will shine through every piece of our brokenness. No, we will never be the same again, we will only shine brighter. We need to surrender our burdens to God, ask for His help in prayer, express forgiveness, and have faith. Spiritual transformation can occur through this process and provides a tremendous source of strength to deal with all the uncertainties of life, including those of cancer.

Consider the healing prayer of Saint Francis of Assisi which follows and take time to reflect on its message. Saint Francis was inspired by God to bring peace, love, and joy to the world. By living this prayer every day of your life, you will feel something deep inside you begin to change. Your heart and the innermost parts of your spirit and soul will grow. Allow the divine love that inspired this wonderful Saint to touch and transform you. This prayer can bring God's love to your heart and spirit so that you can share His love and peace with others in this world.

Prayer of St. Francis of Assisi

Lord, make me an instrument of Your peace.
Where there is hatred, let me sow love;
Where there is injury, pardon;
Where there is doubt, faith;

Where there is despair, hope;
Where there is darkness, light;
Where there is sadness, joy.

Grant that I may not so much seek
To be consoled as to console;
To be understood as to understand;
To be loved as to love.

For it is in giving that we receive;
It is in pardoning that we are pardoned;
And it is in dying that we are born to eternal life.

ST. FRANCIS OF ASSISI (1182-1226)

Lord, make me an instrument of your peace.

Peace on earth needs to start with peace in our own hearts, by thinking and behaving in peaceful ways. We must pray for peace in the world and among all our brothers and sisters regardless of their religion, race or beliefs. When we invite peace into our heart and mind, we partake in the healing of this world. We can only share with others what we have in our own heart and soul.

"Lord, grant me Your peace and help me to choose peace, love and joy, let it start with me."

Where there is hatred, let me sow love;

Healing happens when we open ourselves to the Love of God. We can not heal when we harbor feelings of resentment, hate, and bitterness. We must surrender any feelings, thoughts and actions that are not of love and surrender them over and over again to the Spirit of God.

"Lord, open my heart so I can love deeply without fear."

Where there is injury, pardon;

If we want to be forgiven, we must forgive; the pain inside us can only heal when we forgive the people who have hurt us. Forgiveness is essential for the healing of our mind, body, and spirit. We begin to heal when we begin to love.

"Lord, help me to forgive others and myself."

Where there is doubt, faith;

Doubt, fear, and confusion are not of God. He is the giver of peace, love and joy. We must choose to love, to create peace and to feel the joy of being loved by God. Doubt causes confusion and fear and creates uncertainty. Moving from doubt to faith takes us away from fear.

"Lord, I relinquish my feelings of doubt, I want to trust You, please remove the doubt, confusion and uncertainty from my mind and heart and help me to choose love, peace, and joy."

Where there is despair, hope;

Hope releases energies necessary for our healing. The capacity for Hope is the most significant aspect of the healing process. Hope is created in the mind but lived in the spirit. Without hope we feel despair. Hope is the antidote to despair.

"Lord, help me always to impart hope to others, I want to surrender all my fears and concerns to You and I accept Your will in my life."

Where there is darkness, light;

God's light shines in us; the more we love, the more we shine. God's Spirit shines through you and in you. We can illuminate any darkness and bring light to others who feel darkness, despair, fear, and pain. We can radiate the love of God to everyone we meet.

"Lord, enlighten me and let me be a light in the world and shine wherever there is darkness."

And where there is sadness, joy;

Our tears are the most powerful form of prayer and the most precious to God. Therefore, we must never be ashamed of our tears or hold them back. God wants us to release our sadness and grief to Him. God is the giver of great joy. Live each moment and give each moment in time, let people know what blessings and joys are in your life and pray blessings onto them. With every cross we carry comes a blessing, and with every blessing we give we will be blessed by God. Do not give up believing.

"Lord, help me not to abandon anyone I see in pain, give us joy, for joy in me brings joy to the world."

Grant that I may not so much seek to be consoled as to console;

Love and compassion are the healing balm that touches the human heart and spirit. We can bring healing to others by listening and understanding their pain and burdens. It is the honor, respect, and unconditional love that we have for others that help us to console and walk with them.

"Lord, give me Your strength to be comforting and loving to the people around me."

To be understood, than to understand;

There are things in life we can never fully understand and we don't need to; at times, our logic gets in the way. We must abandon our judgments, expectations and any form of condemnation and try to understand the people around us. We should accept that we all children of God, everyone is unique and no one is perfect. Don't say what is it in them that upsets me; ask what is it in me that causes others to react that way.

"Lord, I relinquish my judgment of others, and any unrealistic expectation I have of people. Help me to change "myself" before I judge and condemn others."

To be loved as to love;

Often we fear love more than desire it. There is no greater power than love. Perfect love heals, accepts, gives, respects, honors, connects, liberates, and ultimately saves us. Love never injures, controls, destroys, calculates, manipulates or deceives. Love is stronger than fear. We must surrender anything that might hinder our ability to be truly and sincerely loving. Open your heart to the beauty and power of God's love.

"Lord, remove all barriers that hinder me to love deeply and fully, open my heart to the greatest power of all, Your love."

For it is in giving that we receive;

Whatever we do and give with love will always return to us. Whatever we do, we do for God. We must give freely and without hidden motives, without expecting something in return. We must look for Christ in the people we encounter in our daily lives, even the difficult ones.

"Lord, help me to serve Your people any way I can, no matter how big or small my contribution, help me to keep Your people in my heart."

It is in pardoning that we are pardoned;

Forgiveness is the key to inner peace and healing. We must forgive if we want to be forgiven. We are forgiven when we love, for love erases many mistakes. Forgiveness will elicit the Spirit to Heal.

"Lord, give me a forgiving heart, help me to let go of all unforgiveness, anger and resentment."

And it is in dying that we are born again;

We can trust in God's promise for eternal life, perfect love, total peace and everlasting joy. The people we love will never leave us, not even death can separate us from their love. For Love is eternal. Relationships are eternal. Our spiritual path will bring us to our eternal home and will unite us with our loved ones forever and ever.

"Lord, in Your hands I place all my doubts, fears and questions; on Your shoulders I place all my burdens. I pray for all my brothers and sisters in this world, may all return to Your divine love. May our minds and hearts be healed. May we all be

blessed. May we find our way home, from pain to peace, from fear to love, from despair to everlasting hope.
Be at my side at the hour of my death and show me the wonders, beauty and glory of Your eternal promise."-- AMEN

CHAPTER 10

The Eternal Spirit

"There is no Death! What seems so is transition;
This life of mortal breath
Is but a suburb of the life elysian,
Whose portal we call Death."

Henry Wadsworth Longfellow (1807 - 1882)

Our spirit lives forever – it is eternal. The spirit is unbounded by the usual limits of our physical body – such as height, weight, age, beauty, disease, even space and time. Our spiritual life is unhindered by these physical laws and constraints which govern the physical universe. Its innate beauty, power, will and essence are limitless. Our spirit provides faith, hope, and strength which cannot be suppressed by the physical forces of our life here on earth.

Making the transition from our physical universe to a spiritual existence is clearly difficult. In fact, change is always difficult in our everyday, physical world. However, we are constantly faced with change in the personal, professional and social aspects of our life. Our natural tendency is to resist change and maintain constancy in our environment. By avoiding change, we continue to exist in a setting that is "known" to us and, in that way, avoid the "unknown." This reaction to avoid the unknown is a mechanism to elude fear, uncertainty, and unpredictability.

But, it is a behavior which is constraining and prevents personal growth, restricts creativity and inhibits true progress. As we mature and learn through experience, we become more flexible and begin to develop ways to deal with change in our life. We realize that we cannot always control our external environment, and we must be flexible and adaptable to meet important changes and challenges that arise during our lifetime. Our success and progress in life can depend upon our ability to adapt to such situations. In the current era of computer technology and global economies, the impetus for each of us to adapt to change is greater than ever before.

Death represents a departure from our physical world, an environment which is known to us. Like change and challenges throughout our life, this exodus from our earthly world heralds new growth and transformation of our spirit. Earlier in this text we discussed the importance of spiritual transformation in meeting the difficult challenges confronting the diagnosis and treatment of cancer. Knowledge and spiritual fortitude lead us down the path of our spiritual journey to complete healing. Near the end of our physical life here on earth, we must make an even greater transition – that from our physical body to the divinely inspired world of our spiritual existence.

In a sense, death is a time of liberation – it represents our freedom from the limits, constraints and maladies of our physical world. After death there is no pain, sickness, weakness or disability. None of the physical burdens which cause us great suffering, hinder our abilities, and impair our existence on earth can affect our spirit. Once our spirit has departed from our body, it is no longer influenced by such worldly phenomena. Our spirit is free to grow and transcends the laws of physics that govern our earth, such as gravity, time and space. Similarly, our spirit is unencumbered by the emotional and psychological traumas which burden so many of our everyday lives. Our spirit enters another dimension, created by God, which is free of these physical, emotional and psychological forces. The spiritual realm is governed by the beauty and splendor of divine Love.

At no time in our existence will we experience a greater transition than death. What is death? Like "commencement" from high school or college, which literally means the beginning of a new phase of life, death represents the beginning of our spiritual existence. Our life on earth has hopefully been a productive and successful learning experience which has prepared us spiritually for this transition. Certainly death is unwelcome as it marks the end of our physical relationship with our family and loved ones. However, death represents a sacred reunion with God and should be celebrated as such. Death is indeed a blessed event of divine creation, not only for patients with cancer, but for all people. After transcending to the realm of our spiritual existence, we will experience unimaginable peace, joy, love and contentment. Based on our faith and our current knowledge of death and near death experiences, we believe our spirit is reunited with God, our family and loved ones whom we have encountered on this earth. The spiritual existence is not lonely or barren or wanting. On the contrary, the spiritual realm is abundant with love, peace and communion with God and others who were so very important in our earthly life.

Cancer confronts us with a challenge of great import – it places our life into perspective and, yes, it reminds us that we are vulnerable. It makes us think profoundly about our life, our loved ones and about our eventual death. We must live everyday to its fullest potential in the awareness that we are loved by God and that life extends beyond our physical existence. God created our life and perpetuates our spiritual existence after our physical life has ended. We are given the opportunity to surrender to God's love in this lifetime so we can be with Him in the next. Henri Nouwen expressed this concept beautifully in his book *Here and Now* (Nouwen HJM, 1994a). We then start to see death in a different light. We realize that death gives us the opportunity to reunite with God and to touch the lives of those whom we have loved and who have loved us. We can bless, touch, teach and even change the lives of others after we leave this life. Our spirit is eternal, it is strong, it is determined, it will go on.

Throughout history, the lives of great men and women became more meaningful after their death. Famous composers, artists, poets and writers often suffered from endless struggles, failures, and physical and mental illness. Yet, they have left many valuable theories, thoughts, and works behind. They continue to shape our way of thinking and often touch our lives more after their death then during their lifetime. The question we need to ask ourselves is "How do I want to be remembered?" To answer this probing question, we must shift our attention from what we have accomplished to who we really are. All people who have lived a spiritual life have chosen to follow God's spirit of love, peace, forgiveness and joy – that spirit will continue to be an everlasting blessing to others. The beauty of God's creation is that our spiritual life can still be meaningful long after our physical life has come to an end. Sons and daughters are deeply aware of the prayers and guidance of their mother long after her death. Through her spirit, she remains in our lives and continues to love, teach and guide us. At times, the love that we feel from our departed mother can be stronger after death than during her lifetime. The strength, resolve and determination of one's father similarly reaches us and continues to impact our daily lives. Our parents continue to be our guardians and to teach us about love and life, humility and sincerity, truthfulness and compassion.

When Christ approached His death, He spoke freely and openly to His closest friends about the end of His earthly life. He acknowledged the sadness and sorrow it would bring. But, His message was one of hope as Christ said that after His death He would send His spirit to stay with us forever. That is why through our death, we bring the Spirit of God to those we leave behind.

By understanding that this deep communion exists even beyond death, we will no longer fear dying and, in fact, have faith and hope in our spiritual existence. We then realize that death does not separate or alienate us – it actually unites us with our loved ones and God. We know that we are born out of love and will die into love – every part of our physical and spiritual being is deeply rooted in love. Our spiritual journey consists of a lifelong search to understand ourselves better, to grow, to learn, and to love others. By gaining this insight, we determine our personal growth and the nature of our relationships with others. God has confidently given us this ability and its associated responsibility. When we stand before God, ready to be reunited with Him in our spiritual existence, what matters most is the way we have lived and expressed love to others. True love resides in our hearts, not in our motives or obligations – divine Love is unconditional. We are not obligated to love but we are created by His love and chosen for love, even beyond the boundaries of our own death. When we care for someone with cancer, we must do it with compassion and tenderness, that is what God's people deserve. To abandon someone who is already hurting and weakened is one of the cruelest acts we can commit against another human being. One who is suffering is precious in the eyes of God and deserves our love. Caring for a dying person is a privilege and honor. Remember, this departure is a sacred transition from the physical to spiritual world. Our love can facilitate this transition and can relieve fear, anxiety and loneliness. We must remind ourselves that we will all be there one day. The ultimate victory is not fighting death, but relieving the feelings of fear, separation, anxiety and abandonment that so often accompany it.

God is with us in every dimension, through every part of our journey, even in our fear of death and dying. No one dies alone. At the moment of our physical departure, we are surrounded by love – the love of our family, loved ones and God. Regardless of the way we die, death is a union of love. Although our physical body departs, our spirit remains eternal. There is no death of our spiritual being, only a sacred transformation. Like a butterfly emerging from its cocoon, our spirit transcends to another dimension. It represents the beginning of another, even more beautiful existence.

Throughout history, we have searched for the answers to profound questions such as: "Why are we here?", "Who am I?", "What is the true meaning of life?", "How do I fit into the universe?", "What happens to us after death?" Philosophers and scholars from ancient and modern religions have debated these questions throughout the history of mankind. We may never be able to completely answer these questions. However, religious and clinical evidence indicates that death is not the end of our existence. To believe that death is not the end, but a transition to an everlasting spiritual life, also takes faith. Faith and belief in our spiritual existence brings us to accept death – and with acceptance comes peace and serenity.

Love is stronger than death. Spiritual union is stronger

than physical separation. Why does death cause so much suffering and pain? It is because we love our family and friends so deeply. We need to use the same emotion that makes us mourn to live in hope – in the hope that we will be reunited with our loved ones and God. Hope and faith are more powerful than fear and uncertainty. Hope disarms fear and faith conquers the unknown. We must remain strong in our convictions and open to the promise of our spiritual existence – despite the fact that we cannot answer all the questions about when, where and how our spiritual transcendence will occur. Despite all of our scientific technology, we may never be able to measure or monitor or conclusively prove life in the spiritual dimension. Our religious and philosophical beliefs, faith and hope are the realities of our spiritual existence.

Love, compassion and faith have the power to conquer the anguish and fear of death. Cancer patients need to know that they our loved and that there is hope for healing beyond this physical life. The deepest and most profound healing we experience is spiritual, not physical. Our spiritual journey is long, in fact, eternal – and only a small fraction of our spiritual life takes place during our physical existence on earth. Death heals us from our physical pain, illusions, hatred and losses. To live without the fear of death is liberating. Our physical departure from this world represents a union of love and faith where our spiritual being will be completed, healed, restored and perfected. Cancer patients often struggle with fears of the unknown, complex medical problems and failing physical health. Finding peace in the midst of these trials can be difficult but is essential to achieve true healing. Peace can only occur when we relinquish anxiety and despair and move to a higher plane of faith, hope and divine Love. We must trust that new life will emerge and feel safe and God's love, knowing that no harm will come to us. It can be difficult to see our own goodness and value when we are stricken with cancer or any severe disease. However, when we are most vulnerable, our spirit radiates the brightest and most beautiful light. Cancer patients exhibit this radiance no matter how physically weak or ill they may be. God's grace is revealed to us in everyone's life and under all conditions. Our greatest suffering can be comforted by God's love on a spiritual level.

One of the most important aspects of our spiritual journey on earth is not what happened to us but what we have learned through our experiences. We must learn to grow spiritually in times of triumph and in defeat, in sickness and in health, in prosperity and in poverty. Healing begins when we surrender to God's love. We must look deep inside our very own nature and transcend worldly constraints to achieve spiritual growth. An important aspect of healing is forgiveness, cleansing our heart from all that hinders us from loving and healing. Retaining hurt and anger has adverse spiritual consequences. Like the laws of gravity on earth, our spiritual force is omnipresent and impels us to love one another and to live in that love daily. When someone we love dies, it is natural for us to experience a sense of loss and deep pain. The intensity of this pain can lead us to a profound connection with that person who is close to our heart. Our deepest self is connected to the core of our loved one, and we are united spiritually by divine Love. The loss of our loved one, therefore, is not destructive but healing – at the all-important spiritual level.

Often people experience depression after the death of one so loved. It feels as if the departed individual has taken part of us away with him. To overcome this feeling of emptiness, we need to surrender that person over to the Love of God. Grief during the mourning process allows us to communicate more deeply with our inner self. It stirs our feelings, fears, and emotions. During this time we need to stay close to God and to remain in His Love daily. Through God we connect with our loved ones who have passed on and with our own spiritual being. We then find strength, not sadness, and a reassurance that our loved ones are safe in God's presence. We also trust and realize that the emptiness we experience in grief is not our final experience and that beyond is a place where all are held and loved forever. With faith in this belief, we realize that our pain, our fears, our anxieties and our grief cannot destroy us. Love, hope, faith and conviction are stronger than fear, uncertainty and death – our spirit will prevail for eternity.

In fact, spiritually we do not belong to this world. We were created and born in God's love and we return to His love after our earthly journey. Both joy and suffering are part of our journey and equally as significant for our spiritual growth. The presence of God is like the air we breathe, the sun's rays on a brilliant day, the force of gravity – He is omnipresent. But we must never take His presence for granted. His love is the greatest and most precious gift imaginable.

Our death represents a return to the One who loves us unconditionally. Our spirit thrives in God's love and can only reach its full potential in that dimension. We may then understand the purpose of our spiritual journey on earth. Our faith tells us that there is nothing to fear as death is an act of divine Love – one that leads us to eternal communion with God and the people we love forever. We must remain hopeful and believe that our brief journey on this earth will continue to touch, bless and enrich the lives of others. Once we are released from our mortal bodies, we are free to soar and to spiritually grow.

Our spirit will continue to live within our loved ones who remain on this earth.

Anxiety-producing thoughts about death can be very harmful to our psyche. How can we deal with such thoughts and feelings productively? When a fearful thought, restlessness, physical pain, or emotions of fear or anxiety arise, do not withdraw or immediately repress them. Experience that anxious or painful feeling for a moment or two and allow the pain to create your prayer. Let tears come forth and realize that your tears are one of the most precious forms of prayer. Let your pain direct the intentions of your prayer. Then, release your pain to God. Painful emotions and even some physical pains resolve when fully accepted, expressed and released in this way. Have faith and allow the strength of your prayer to heal your suffering. The purpose of prayer is not to experience immediate peace but to release anxiety and painful emotions to God. Our spirit becomes stronger. The release creates peace and tranquility. If these feelings of sadness, anxiety and restlessness recur, accept them and then release them again to God. Our usual response to pain is one of withdrawal or denial – but nothing is more stressful to our body or mind than avoiding emotional pain. Our body and spirit suffer when we retain unresolved issues which cause pain. By accepting our emotions, visualizing God's presence, and releasing our pain to God, our spirit is strengthened. By confronting our feelings in this way, we can disarm fear and be relieved of our suffering.

Besides prayer, other noetic techniques can be used with success to strengthen our spiritual resolve and essence. For example, meditation, yoga, music, art, architecture and a return to nature are other common mechanisms to promote physical and spiritual well-being. Our incredible patient Sister Rose clearly

156

uses prayer as an important resource to strengthen her own spirit and that of others. She is also an award-winning nature photographer and remains active in that capacity at 81 years of age. The goal of her efforts is to capture the glory, beauty and wonder of God's creation on this earth for all to experience through her photographs. Her photographs are healing for others and are now displayed in hospitals and cancer centers for that reason – but, nature photography is also healing for her and brings her even closer to God through her connection with His creations.

We each have a unique spirituality. Like our personality, our fingerprints or our genetic makeup, our spiritual life is unique and distinguishes us from others. Likewise, there are many techniques and mechanisms for achieving spiritual growth. The individuality and creativity of each person's spirituality should be encouraged. There are no right or wrong ways to grow spiritually. The only certainty is that our transcendence from the physical to the spiritual world will occur. Our Creator has provided us with different abilities and mechanisms to achieve our spiritual growth and transformation. In His wisdom, He has given us the ability to understand our spiritual existence and to achieve spiritual healing. He has given us the tremendous capacity to embrace faith and hope – He does not leave us alone or abandoned. Consider the following prayer from Saint Padre Pio and reflect on its meaning for a few moments:

Stay with me Lord,
For it is necessary to have You present
So that I do not forget You.

Stay with me Lord,
Because I am so weak and I need Your strength
So that I may not fall so often.

Stay with me Lord,
For You are my life.
And without You, I am without fervor.

Stay with me Lord,
For You are my light,
And without You I am in darkness.

Stay with me Lord,
So that I hear Your voice and follow You.

Stay with me Lord,
For I desire to love You very much,
And always be in Your company.

Stay with me Lord,
If You wish me to be faithful to You.

Stay with me Lord,
For as poor as my soul is,
I wanted to be a place of consolation for You,
A nest of love. – Amen

Saint Padre Pio (1887 - 1968)

We now have faith that our physical departure from this earth is a sacred event in the journey of our spiritual existence. With true faith and conviction, there is no place for fear or anxiety. Our spirit clearly feels no fear or anxiety and must transcend from this physical world and return to its spiritual home. Only then can our spiritual being be reunited with God and our loved ones. Our spirit is destined to undergo this blessed transformation, one which is created, nurtured and maintained in God's love. Our spirit is eternal.

CHAPTER 11

PRAYER IS POWERFUL

"Prayer is the most powerful form of energy one can
generate. The influence of prayer on the human mind
and body is as demonstrable as that of the secreting
glands. Prayer is a force as real as terrestrial gravity.
It supplies us with a flow of sustaining power in our
daily lives."

Alexis Carrel (1873 – 1944)

Ancient man used spirituality and religion to achieve
healing thousands of years before history was recorded. The
joining of spirituality, religion and health was practiced in
disparate cultures and peoples located in remote areas scattered
across the earth. There were no telephones, telegraphs, radio or
television broadcasts, postal service or e-mail available for these
ancient cultures to communicate. Yet, our prehistoric ancestors
from varied backgrounds and cultures recognized the healing
power of spirituality and religion.

As science progressed throughout history, scientists
increasingly relied on direct observation and experimentation and
less on faith and religious doctrine to explain our physical world.
Astronomy, physics, biology and medicine began to diverge from
religious beliefs – secretly at first and then openly and defiantly.
The greatest challenge to the Church occurred in the 16th and 17th

centuries when Copernicus and Galileo provided evidence that the earth revolved around the sun (Webster C,1975). The earth, and therefore man, was no longer the center of the universe – this concept literally turned the universe upside down and widened a chiasm that had been developing between science and religion for centuries.

Should science remain purely secular, independent of religion and spirituality? Can religion survive isolated from and ignoring scientific discovery? No, neither science nor religion can stand alone. Scientific inquiry and religion, theology, and spirituality are clearly inter-related and are now beginning to be re-united. Science and religion are both needed to even begin to understand the most significant questions of our time, such as the origin of life, the creation and evolution of the universe, the concepts of space and time, and the nature of the human spirit, to name only a few.

Today, we have the tremendous opportunity to combine the power of spirituality with the modern technology of conventional medicine. Medicine and spirituality are becoming more integrated in recent years as patients' health problems increasingly involve spiritual and religious concerns. Clinical medicine clearly has limitations and the vast majority of patients today believe that spirituality can play an important role in the healing process. Like the covert beginnings of the scientific revolution which occurred centuries ago, the use of spirituality and religion for healing by patients is commonly concealed from their treating physicians. However, even the attitude of practicing medical physicians is beginning to change. In fact, many primary care physicians now recognize the influence and clinical relevance between spiritual well being and physical health. Yet, a dichotomy exists between current medical practice and the belief that spirituality can impact clinical medicine.

Nowhere does the union of spirituality and medicine have more to offer than in the treatment of cancer. Cancer is feared worldwide because of its uncertainty of cure, its unpredictability for recurrence, and its potential to threaten our life. Our basic human survival instinct is challenged by this disease – which affects us physically, emotionally, psychologically and spiritually. A crisis of faith can occur and accentuate feelings of anger, frustration, despair and hopelessness in the cancer patient. These destructive feelings can be relieved by invoking spirituality to improve one's quality of life and to enhance the coping mechanisms of the patient and his family and caregivers.

Spirituality is unique for each individual and provides a tremendous resource capable of affecting one's physical health. Through the mind-body-spirit connection, spirituality can reduce stress, anxiety, fear, and depression and augment one's physical and emotional health. Spirituality is a complex and mysterious phenomenon which is distinct from religion, but can certainly include one's religion. Spirituality embodies faith in a Greater Power, trust, hope, prayer, meditation, personal transformation, and the meaning or purpose of life. One's spirituality can be dramatically strengthened by spiritually based therapy and empowered to confront the most difficult challenges of our life.

Healing prayer is a vital part of Spiritual Integrated Therapy that can help access spiritual resources and provide support to overcome the problems facing many cancer patients. Prayer is powerful and is our way of communicating directly with God. During prayer God touches our soul and spirit with His love and strength. Prayer is divine energy that we can access any time and anywhere – it is as definite and forceful as gravity or electricity or magnetism. Prayer is like an inner fire that enlightens our spirit, a spiritual lifeline to God. In the act of prayer, we can ask, seek and find guidance, strength and inspiration from the grace of God. In prayer, we are free to surrender our feelings, burdens, problems and emotions to God. There is tremendous power in opening our heart to God in prayer – a power that cannot be precisely measured and that may always remain somewhat mysterious to us. Nevertheless, we can capture God's love in our heart and progress along our unique, divinely inspired path to healing.

Our path to true healing requires spiritual awareness and personal transformation. We must be open to the power of prayer and spirituality. By combining the power of prayer with conventional medicine, we have the potential to attain true healing of our physical, emotional and spiritual being. Spiritual Integrated Therapy combines the healing forces of the human body, mind and spirit with the power and love of God. We believe that all healing ultimately comes from God and that healing prayer can release forces to complete and support standard medical treatment of diseases such as cancer. The purpose and essence of this therapy is to open one to the unlimited love, power and grace of God and to affirm that we are not alone in times of struggle and illness.

Throughout history, there are stories of extraordinary individuals who give us hope and courage in our own battles with adversity. Against overwhelming circumstances and challenges, these remarkable people met their challenges with hope, faith and determination and left behind a legacy of glory. One of these incredible individuals is Michelangelo, one of the greatest artistic geniuses of all time. Despite his ability and achievements, Michelangelo led a tremendously tormented life. He suffered from many physical and emotional hardships and was constantly searching for a deeper meaning and significance of his life. Despite his personal conflicts, he was able to create magnificent works of art, usually during the most traumatic times of his life. While painting the ceiling of the Sistine Chapel, Michelangelo suffered from the abandonment of his family and friends, the early death of his mother, the hatred of his rivals, and the loneliness of his heart. He ultimately suffered a deep spiritual crisis, feeling totally abandoned and unloved by God. He secluded himself from the world, and his only escape was his work. But, he was not abandoned by God – in fact, his artistic expression was inspired by the Spirit of God. When everything in his physical world failed him, God's divine Spirit stayed with him. God's Spirit moved through him and inspired his eyes and his hands to create perhaps the most wonderful spiritual masterpieces ever known in this world. What Michelangelo captured was the essence of creation inspired in him by God Himself. His physical pain and afflictions were so great that he was unable to feel or sense God's guidance and inspiration – in fact, the source of his spiritual despair was the feeling that God had abandoned him. But his work clearly demonstrates the power of God helping him to access his divine gift of creativity despite his suffering. Michelangelo was one of those heroic individuals who never stopped battling his worldly challenges and was richly rewarded spiritually (Orlandi E, 1966).

Spiritual Integrated Therapy aims to facilitate personal growth and transformation during the most challenging times of our life. This spiritually oriented approach has unique resources for dealing with human brokenness, suffering and despair, all commonly seen in cancer patients. Patients open to this approach can experience God's love as a life-changing process and can acquire strength to endure those difficult challenges. The resources and benefits of Spiritual Integrated Therapy have the potential to go far beyond that of conventional techniques of psychotherapy, which focus primarily on healing forces within the patient. The spiritual integrated approach promotes healing at multiple levels, including the physical, emotional, psychological and spiritual realms.

True healing is accomplished when we learn to accept God's love and grace, forgiveness and the transformation of our spirit and soul through the presence of God. The Spirit of God provides us with a tremendous source of wisdom, strength, inspiration and insight. We can develop spiritual strength regardless and independent of our physical, mental and emotional health. The spiritual strength that we develop during Spiritual Integrated Therapy is lasting and is, perhaps, our deepest form of healing. We can be sustained through the power of prayer and by surrendering our circumstances, struggles and burdens to God. Forgiveness is part of the healing process offered by this treatment approach. Release of resentment, anger, and bitterness facilitates the healing process and brings peace to our heart, mind and soul.

Prayer connects us to the Spirit of God. Healing prayer is a release of our fearful, sad or angry thoughts and feelings to God – otherwise, they can negatively affect our physical, emotional and spiritual well-being. By releasing these emotions in prayer, our body and mind can return to tranquility and balance. We can experience a greater sense of peacefulness and well-being – nothing is more tranquil and serene than to be in the divine presence of God's Spirit. Healing prayer can remove us from the flow of ordinary thoughts and allow us to enter our deeper, inner self. This form of prayer opens us to our spiritual essence. We can then relinquish our anxious thoughts to God and allow these thoughts to flow out of us like a stream. By connecting our mind, our heart and our spirit to God in prayer, we can surrender our fears, anxiety, pain and loneliness to Him. Illness, such as cancer, provides us with the opportunity to release these negative feelings and to strengthen and heal our spirit.

Spiritual Integrated Therapy can open us to the concept of spiritual awareness and personal transformation. We can invite God into our healing process to turn our weaknesses to strength, our challenges to glory and our struggles to peace. We must move beyond anger, frustration and despair to acceptance, compassion and faith. Transformation is not the end result of our spiritual journey – it is the process of our healing journey and the way in which we become spiritually renewed. Spirituality helps us to enhance the creative capacity and insight in all areas of our life. God inspires us when we begin to open ourselves to His Spirit. His inspiration can flow through us and create a new excitement for art, music, literature and nature. Our spiritual eyes open to the beauty and wonder of God's creation, and we perceive His world and people in greater depth than ever before.

Part of our spiritual journey is to realize that we are not alone. The Spirit of God is with us always and helps us through the most difficult times of our life. Saint Paul described nine aspects of spiritual life that resemble the Presence of God's Spirit: love, joy, peace, patience, kindness, goodness, faithfulness, gentleness, and self-control (Gal 5: 22-23). By living these attributes along our spiritual journey, we can achieve personal transformation and true spiritual healing. Just as important, we can express love and compassion to all of God's people around us. When we live a spiritual life, we allow God's Spirit to live through us. He will guide us, and those who exhibit these superb spiritual qualities radiate and shine with His Presence. No other energy is as healing and powerful as that of divine love and kindness.

We are always connected to God and to those He has sent to walk with us on our spiritual path. God brings people into our lives to encourage, teach, love and support us as we make important life decisions and choices. We also have spiritual guidance from loved ones who have departed this earth and from our guardian angel whom God has placed beside us. To hope is to believe that God can do things that we cannot and to trust in the mystery and power of divine intervention. Through this healing process, we learn to maintain our hope, faith and trust that God will give us the strength to overcome our difficult life challenges.

We are spiritually revitalized when we awaken to the love of God. Spiritual Integrated Therapy can be a life-changing and transforming process which is divinely inspired. By developing our spiritual strength, we become aware of the needs of others whom we can comfort, as they comfort us. The human spirit has unlimited potential to provide us and those around us with hope, faith, peace and serenity. Our spiritual resources provide an important source of spiritual wisdom and strength at the most difficult moments of our life. Thomas Keating, a Cistercian priest and founder of the centering prayer movement in Colorado, teaches that the presence of the Spirit of God is like oxygen, we can never escape from it (Keating T, 1986). God's Spirit allows us to release our stress and burdens and surrender them to Him. By doing so, we can experience profound peace and tranquility in our life. To experience such peace is a form of enlightenment created by our personal awareness and spiritual union with God. Prayer opens us to the spiritual dimension of our being and forms a sacred connection to God.

The process of inner healing involves every part of our body, mind, emotions and spirit. Prayer, meditation and other spiritual activities reconnect us to the loving Spirit of God, the life force of our being and the divine energy and light of our life. Healing prayer brings divine forces together in such a powerful way that fears and anxieties are calmed, hope and faith flourish, and peace dominates. During prayer we are in direct contact with God. By praying for another, we can surrender the situation and that person to the divine love of God, and pray that He will touch their lives in ways we never could. Through prayer, we can express our love and surrender His people and their needs to God. In prayer we connect the heart of God with the person for whom we pray. You can even let your last thoughts at night remain in prayer and, by the Grace of God, your sleep will be a constant prayer to Him. This type of simple prayer can lead to deep healing of our heart, body, mind and spirit.

Conventional medicine has limitations – medications cannot release emotional trauma, and surgery cannot remove resentment, fear and despair. These emotional, psychological and spiritual burdens can be released in prayer so that healing can occur. Our spiritual journey is a path that can awaken our spirit to the love and guidance of God. Our spiritual growth and transformation is a process which takes time – it is not an instantaneous phenomenon. We must have hope, faith and trust in God and surrender our burdens to Him. God never abandons us and through our prayers, we can always communicate with Him. One of the most beautiful descriptions of God's unconditional love and His knowledge of us is eloquently expressed in the Psalm of David. This divine love story makes us aware that we are unique and precious to God and that He has chosen each one of us to be part of this world. This Psalm relates one of the mysteries of life – that God can search our heart and show us what we need to change. This is precisely what the spiritual integrated approach encourages. Reflect on the Psalm of David for a few moments and let it speak to your heart.

PSALM 139

Lord, You have examined my heart and know everything about me.
You know when I sit down or stand up.
You know my every thought when far away.
You chart the path ahead of me and tell me where to stop and rest.
Every moment You know where I am.
You know what I am going to say even before I say it, Lord.
You both precede and follow me. You place Your hand of blessing on my head.
Such knowledge is too wonderful for me, too great for me to know!

I can never escape from Your spirit! I can never get away from Your presence!
If I go up to heaven, You are there; if I go down to the place of the dead, You are there.
If I ride the wings of the morning, if I dwell by the farthest oceans, even there You will guide me, and Your strength will support me. I could ask the darkness to hide me and the light around me to become night – but even in darkness I cannot hide from You.

To You the night shines as bright as the day. Darkness and light are both alike to You.

You made all the delicate, inner parts of my body and knit me together in my mother's womb. Thank You for making me so wonderfully complex!
Your workmanship is marvelous – and how well I know it.
You watched me as I was being formed in utter seclusion,
as I was woven together in the dark of the womb.
You saw me before I was born. Every day of my life was recorded in Your book.
Every moment was laid out before a single day had passed.

How precious are Your thoughts about me, O God! They are innumerable!
I can't count them; they outnumber the grains of sand!
And when I wake up in the morning You are still with me!

Search me, O God, and know my heart; test me and know my thoughts.
Point out anything in me that offends You, and lead me along the path of everlasting life.

PSALM OF DAVID

Our spirit is unbounded by the laws and limits of our physical world. The human spirit has tremendous healing potential and is eternal. Although death marks our physical departure from this world, it also represents our spiritual freedom from such burdens as fear, pain, anxiety and depression. Our spirit can transcend these worldly burdens and enter into another dimension, created by God. Our spiritual journey is destined to take us back to our Creator – a sacred reunion made of divine love and inspiration.

God provides us with the strength and courage to overcome any challenge or burden which we might encounter on this earth. With faith, hope and prayer, the Spirit of God guides us as we progress along our spiritual journey. During the most difficult and seemingly darkest moments of our life, He is there to illuminate the way for us. We are never alone, we are never abandoned by God. Our ultimate destiny is to reunite with our divine Creator in a spiritual realm that is eternal. Along our journey, our divinely inspired prayers can relieve our worldly burdens and create the **spirit to heal.**

REFERENCES

Baker IA. 1997. The Tibetian Art of Healing. San Francisco. Chronicle Books.

Barry J. 1987. French Lovers. New York. Arbor House.

Braunwald E, Hauser SL, Fauci AS, et al. 2001. Harrison's Principles of Internal Medicine (15th edition). New York. McGraw-Hill.

Carmichael AG, Ratzan RM (eds). 1991. Medicine: A Treasury of Art and Literature. New York. Hugh Lauter Levin Associates, Inc.

Cousins N (ed). 1996. The Words of Albert Schweitzer. Westminster. New Market Press.

Davidson CN. 1996. The Book of Love, Writers and their Love Letters. New York. Plume/Penguin.

Dossey L. 1993. Healing Words. New York. Harper Collins.

Eckhart M. 1981. The Essential Sermons, Commentaries, Treatises, and Defenses. New York. Paulist Press.

Ellis H. 2001. A History of Surgery. London. Greenwich Medical Media Limited.

Engel GL. 1977. The need for a new medical model; a challenge to biomedicine. Science 196: 129 – 136.

Frankl VE. 1980. The Doctor and the Soul. New York. Random House, Inc.

Frankl VE. 1992. Man's Search for Meaning. Boston. Beacon Press.

General Assembly of the United Nations. 1948. Universal declaration of human rights. Geneva, Switzerland.

Givner J. 1982. Catherine Ann Porter; A Life. New York. Simon and Schuster.

Grmek MD. 1991. Diseases in the Ancient Greek World. Baltimore. Johns Hopkins University Press.

Guyton AC, Hall JE. 2000. Textbook of Medical Physiology (10th edition). Philadelphia. W.B. Saunders Company.

Hirai T. 1974. Psychophysiology of Zen. Tokyo. Igaku Shoin.

Kaczorowski JM. 1989. Spiritual well-being and anxiety levels in adults diagnosed with cancer. Hospice Journal 5: 105 – 116.

Keating T. 1986. Open Mind, Open Heart. New York. The Continuum Publishing Co.

Keating T. 1996. Invitation to Love. New York. The Continuum Publishing Co.

Killorin J (ed). 1978. Selected Letters to Conrad Aiken. New Haven. Yale University Press.

King DE, Bushwick B. 1994. Beliefs and attitudes of hospital inpatients about faith healing and prayer. Journal of Family Practice 39: 349 – 352.

King DE, Sobel J, Haggerty J, et al. 1992. Experiences and attitudes about faith healing among family physicians. Journal of Family Practice 35: 158 – 162.

Kipple KF (ed). 1993. The Cambridge World History of Human Disease. Cambridge. Cambridge University Press.

Klein S, Tracy D, Kitchener HC, Walker LG. 2000. The effects of the participation of patients with cancer in teaching communication skills to medical undergraduates; a randomised study with follow-up after 2 years. European Journal of Cancer 36: 273 – 281.

Keubler-Ross E. 1991. Life After Death. Berkeley. Celestialarts.

Lown B. 1996. The Lost Art of Healing. New York. Ballantine Books.

MacLeod R. 2001. Learning from Sir William Osler about the teaching of palliative care. Journal of Palliative Care 17: 265 – 269.

Magner LN. 1992. A History of Medicine. New York. Marcel Dekker, Inc.

Mead FS. 1965. 12,000 Inspirational Quotations; A Treasury of Spiritual Insights and Practical Wisdom. Springfield. Federal Street Press. Selected quotations reprinted with permission at the beginning of each chapter.

Moore T. 1994. Soul Mates. New York. Harper Perennial.

Mueller PS, Plevak DJ, Rummans TA. 2001. Religious involvement, spirituality and medicine; implications for clinical practice. Mayo Clinic Proceedings 76: 1225 – 1235.

Newberg A, D'aquili E, Rause V. 2001. <u>Why God Won't Go Away</u>. New York. The Ballantine Publishing Group.

Nouwen HJM. 1992a. <u>Life of the Beloved</u>. New York. The Crossroad Publishing Co.

Nouwen HJM. 1992b. <u>Who Are We? Exploring Our Christian Identity</u>. Notre Dame. Ave Maria Press.

Nouwen HJM. 1994a. <u>Here and Now</u>. New York. The Crossroad Publishing Co.

Nouwen HJM. 1994b. <u>The Inner Voice of Love</u>. New York. Image Books.

Orlandi E. 1966. <u>The Life, Times and Art of Michelangelo</u>. New York. Crescent Books.

Pappas S, Perlman A. 2002. Complementary and alternative medicine; the importance of doctor-patient communication. Medical Clinics of North America 86: 1 – 10.

Porter R. 1997. <u>The Greatest Benefit to Mankind; A Medical History of Humanity</u>. New York. W.W. Norton and Company.

Reeves C. 1992. <u>Egyptian Medicine</u>. Princess Risborough. Shire Publications.

Roth R, Occhiogrosso P. 1997. <u>The Healing Path of Prayer</u>. New York. Three River Press.

Sandford J, Sandford P. 1982. <u>The Transformation of the Inner Man</u>. Tulsa. Victory House.

Sandford J, Sandford P. 1985. Healing of the Wounded Spirit. Tulsa. Victory House.

Scudder H. 1899. The Complete Poetical Works of John Keats. Cambridge. The Riverside Press.

Sephton SE, Koopman C, Schaal M, et al. 2001. Spiritual expression and immune status in women with metastatic breast cancer; an exploratory study. Breast Journal 7: 345 – 353.

Sloan RP, Bagiella E, Powell T. 1999. Religion, spirituality and medicine. Lancet 353: 664 – 667.

Suplee C. 2000. Milestones of Science. Washington, D.C. National Geographic.

Wear A, French R, Loine I (eds). 1985. The Medical Renaissance of the Sixteenth Century. Cambridge. Cambridge University Press.

Webster C. 1975. The Great Instauration: Science, Medicine and Reform 1626-1660. London. Duckworth.

Wilkinson BH, Kirk PA, Hoover JW (eds). 1997. The Daily Walk Bible; New Living Translation. Wheaton. Tyndale House Publishers, Inc. Selected scripture quotations reprinted from the Holy Bible, New Living Translation copyright © 1996.

Williamson M. 1992. A Return to Love. New York. Harper Collins.

More Inspirational Books From:

Dr. Michael Torosian & Dr. Veruschka Biddle

SPIRIT TO HEAL
A Journey to Spiritual Healing with Cancer
$ 15.95 ISBN 0-9729419-0-8

SPIRIT TO HEAL – JOURNAL OF PRAYER
$ 10.95 ISBN 0-9729419-1-6

Additional Books Coming Soon, Including:

RESTA CON ME SIGNORE – Stay with me Lord
$ 10.95 ISBN 0-9729419-2-4

To order by mail, send payment (check, credit card number/
expiration date, or money order) plus S&H payable to:
Spirit Press International

Your order will be processed immediately if books are available,
otherwise please allow 5-6 weeks for delivery

SPIRIT PRESS INTERNATIONAL
P.O. BOX 544
WAYNE, PA 19087

Please visit our website for more information, including
upcoming seminars, workshops, lectures and retreats.

www.spirittoheal.com